GCSE English

The Sign of the Four

by Arthur Conan Doyle

Hidden treasure! Murder! High-speed steamboat chases! *The Sign of the Four* is certainly exciting, but you'll need to stay calm to write top essays about it.

Fortunately, this brilliant Text Guide explains everything you'll need — characters, language, structure, themes… the lot. And because it's a CGP book, we get straight to the point, with no needless rambling.

We've also included plenty of practice questions to test you on what you've learned, plus a section of advice on how to plan and write brilliant answers in the exam. It doesn't take Sherlock Holmes to deduce that it's a steal.

The Text Guide

CONTENTS

CONTENTS

Section Four — Themes

Section Five — The Writer's Techniques

Section Six — Exam Advice

The Characters in 'The Sign of the Four'
'The Sign of the Four' Cartoon

Published by CGP

Editors:
Claire Boulter
Emma Cleasby
Alex Fairer

Contributor:
Anna Hall

With thanks to Sean Walsh and Elisabeth Quincey for the proofreading.
With thanks to Ana Pungartnik for the copyright research.

Acknowledgements:

Cover image © Aleksandra Lech (https://aleksandralech.artstation.com)

With thanks to Alamy for permission to use the images on pages 1, 6, 7, 8, 24 & 53.

With thanks to Mary Evans Picture Library for permission to use the image on page 2.

With thanks to Rex Features for permission to use the images on pages 3, 4, 10, 11, 12, 14, 16, 17, 19, 26, 28, 30, 31, 34, 35, 41, 43, 48 & 51.

With thanks to Chris Wooley for permission to use the images on page 3, 4, 5, 13, 15, 18, 20, 21, 25, 27, 29, 32, 33, 38, 39, 44, 45, 49, 52 & 54.

With thanks to ArenaPAL for permission to use the images on pages 5, 40, 42 & 50.

With thanks to Photostage.co.uk for permission to use the image on page 5.

Every effort has been made to locate copyright holders and obtain permission to reproduce sources.
For those sources where it has been difficult to trace the copyright holder of the work, we would be grateful
for information. If any copyright holder would like us to make an amendment to the acknowledgements,
please notify us and we will gladly update the book at the next reprint. Thank you.

ISBN: 978 1 78294 853 7
Printed by Elanders Ltd, Newcastle upon Tyne.
Images and Clipart throughout the book from Corel® and Clipart.com.

Based on the classic CGP style created by Richard Parsons.

Introducing 'The Sign of the Four' and Conan Doyle

'The Sign of the Four' is a mystery story

- *The Sign of the Four* is set in the 19th century. It features the private detective Sherlock Holmes and his friend Dr John Watson. In the novel, they investigate a mystery involving murder and stolen treasure.

- Holmes is very intelligent. He doesn't rely on chance or luck to solve cases — he uses science and logic.

Science in 19th-Century Britain

© World History Archive / Alamy Stock Photo

1) The Victorian period saw rapid scientific progress.

2) Many new discoveries were made in fields such as medicine, forensics and chemistry.

3) Science became a profession, and many ordinary people became more interested in science.

4) Scientists used observation, experimentation and analysis of evidence to prove their theories.

Conan Doyle had a medical background

- Arthur Conan Doyle studied medicine and practised as a doctor before finding success as a writer.

- His main inspiration for Holmes was one of his university professors, Dr Joseph Bell. He was impressed by how Bell could arrive at accurate conclusions by making detailed observations of his patients.

- Conan Doyle wrote 4 novels and 56 short stories featuring Holmes, who became a very popular character. He tried to kill off Holmes in 1893, but a public outcry persuaded him to bring Holmes back.

1859	Born in Edinburgh.
1876	Went to Edinburgh University to study medicine.
1882	Opened his own medical practice in Portsmouth. Divided his time between medicine and writing.
1887	His first novel featuring Sherlock Holmes, 'A Study in Scarlet', was published.
1890	'The Sign of the Four' was published.
1891	Gave up medicine to concentrate on writing.
1892	'The Adventures of Sherlock Holmes', a collection of short stories, was published.
1902	Knighted for his book about the Boer War.
1930	Died, aged 71.

Background Information

'The Sign of the Four' is set in London and India

Here are the <u>key locations</u> in the novel:

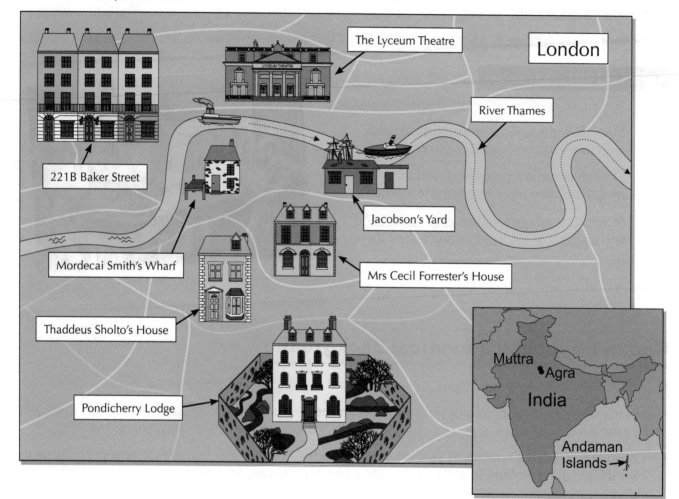

The Lyceum Theatre

London

River Thames

221B Baker Street

Jacobson's Yard

Mordecai Smith's Wharf

Mrs Cecil Forrester's House

Thaddeus Sholto's House

Pondicherry Lodge

Muttra

Agra

India

Andaman Islands →

Catching criminals was difficult in 19th-Century England

- The novel is set in the late 1880s, when London was policed by the <u>Metropolitan Police Force</u> — also known as <u>Scotland Yard</u>. Its main job was to keep <u>order</u> in the capital.

- However, <u>crimes</u> also needed to be <u>investigated</u> and <u>solved</u>. A small <u>detective force</u> was set up in 1842, and this was <u>expanded</u> into the <u>Criminal Investigation Department</u> in 1878.

- These detectives had some success, but they often lacked the <u>information</u> they needed to <u>confidently</u> catch the right person — <u>forensic techniques</u> were in their <u>early stages</u>, so many <u>clues</u> at crime scenes were <u>missed</u>.

- In Sherlock Holmes, Conan Doyle created a detective who could <u>accurately</u> solve crimes using <u>scientific</u> techniques. Holmes carefully <u>examines</u> crime scenes and collects <u>evidence</u>, which allows him to state his theories with <u>certainty</u> — and he's nearly always shown to be <u>right</u>.

Who's Who in 'The Sign of the Four'

Sherlock Holmes...

...is a hugely talented private detective. He loves solving cases but is often emotionally cold towards other people.

Dr John Watson...

...is the novel's narrator and a former army doctor. He lives with Holmes and is his closest friend.

Mary Morstan...

...is a young governess who asks Holmes for help. She's kind and brave, and Watson is attracted to her.

Athelney Jones...

...is a police inspector. He sees Holmes as a rival, but he is far less skilled than Holmes and makes mistakes.

Major Sholto...

...is a retired army officer. He is greedy and is prepared to cheat others to gain wealth.

Captain Morstan...

...is Mary's father. He served in the army with Major Sholto but went missing ten years ago.

Thaddeus Sholto...

...is a wealthy, eccentric man who wants to help Mary. He is the son of Major Sholto.

Bartholomew Sholto...

...is Thaddeus's twin brother. He is selfish and doesn't agree with Thaddeus that they should help Mary.

Jonathan Small...

...is a ruthless, cunning ex-convict. He used to be a soldier in India, and he has a wooden leg.

Tonga...

...is Small's accomplice. He is a native of the Andaman Islands and is extremely loyal to Small.

Introduction

'The Sign of the Four' — Plot Summary

'The Sign of the Four'... what happens when?

Here's a quick recap of the main events of *The Sign of the Four*. Mystery stories can be tricky to follow, but this summary will help you get your head around the plot. It's no substitute for reading the novel though.

Chapters 1 to 3 — A case for Holmes

- Holmes and Watson are at their house, 221B Baker Street, when Mary Morstan arrives to ask Holmes for help.

- Mary explains that her father, Captain Morstan, disappeared ten years ago in London while on leave from the army. The only person in town who knew him was Major Sholto.

- Mary reveals that, for the past six years, an anonymous person has been sending her pearls in the post. She shows Holmes a letter asking her to be at the Lyceum Theatre at 7pm that evening. Holmes and Watson agree to go with her.

- On the way to the theatre, Mary reveals that her father and Major Sholto were stationed together on the Andaman Islands. She shows Holmes a piece of paper from her father's desk — it has a plan of a building on it and the words "The sign of the four" with four names.

- They arrive at the theatre and are met by a coachman who drives them to a house in South London.

Chapters 4 to 6 — The case deepens

- Holmes, Watson and Mary meet Thaddeus Sholto, the son of Major Sholto. Thaddeus explains that his father and Captain Morstan acquired treasure in India. Thaddeus then reveals that Morstan died of a heart attack during an argument over how to split the treasure, and Major Sholto kept it all. On his deathbed, Major Sholto told his sons, Thaddeus and Bartholomew, that he felt guilty for not sharing it with Mary.

- Holmes learns that Major Sholto was about to tell his sons the treasure's location when the Major saw a man at the window and died from shock. On the same night, someone ransacked the Major's room and left a note reading "The sign of the four".

- Thaddeus reveals that he sent Mary the pearls and that his brother Bartholomew has now found the rest of the treasure. They go to Bartholomew's house, Pondicherry Lodge, but discover that he has been killed. Another "sign of the four" note has been left, and the treasure has gone.

- Inspector Athelney Jones arrives and arrests Thaddeus for murder. However, Holmes believes that the real culprits are a man named Jonathan Small and an accomplice.

- Holmes asks Watson to collect a dog called Toby, who he thinks will be able to track the criminals.

Introduction

Chapters 7 to 10 — Holmes closes in on the culprits

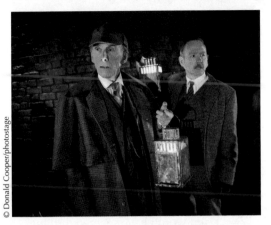

- Toby picks up the <u>trail</u> of Small and his accomplice, and Holmes and Watson <u>follow</u> him.

- Holmes explains his theory — Small was a <u>convict</u> on the <u>Andaman Islands</u>, he <u>told</u> Sholto and Morstan about the <u>treasure</u>, but they <u>double-crossed</u> him and he wanted <u>revenge</u>.

- Toby leads Holmes and Watson to a <u>landing stage</u> (dock). They learn that Small hired a boat called the <u>Aurora</u>.

- Holmes asks the <u>Baker Street irregulars</u>, a group of young boys, to help him <u>find</u> the boat.

- Two days pass with <u>no news</u> of the boat, so Holmes goes to look for it <u>himself</u>. Later that day, <u>Athelney Jones</u> comes to Baker Street after receiving a message from <u>Holmes</u> that says he is <u>closing in</u> on the culprits. Jones reveals that Thaddeus has an <u>alibi</u> and has been released.

- A man in <u>seafaring clothes</u> arrives at Baker Street, claiming to <u>know</u> where the boat and the treasure are — it turns out to be Holmes in <u>disguise</u>. Holmes asks Jones to provide a <u>police boat</u> for that evening.

- They travel by boat to <u>Jacobson's yard</u>, where Small has <u>hidden</u> the Aurora.

- The Aurora emerges and speeds off. The police boat <u>chases</u> it, and Holmes and Watson <u>shoot</u> Small's accomplice. Small is <u>captured</u> and the <u>treasure chest</u> is retrieved from his boat.

Chapters 11 to 12 — The case is solved

- Watson takes the treasure chest to <u>Mary</u>, but it is <u>empty</u> — Small has thrown the treasure into the <u>river</u>.

- Small explains how he became part of 'the four' in <u>India</u>. He helped three men to murder another man in return for a share of the treasure he was carrying. 'The four' were <u>arrested</u> and imprisoned on the <u>Andaman Islands</u>, where Small <u>met</u> Sholto and Morstan.

- Small promised Sholto and Morstan a <u>share</u> of the treasure if they <u>freed</u> him and the other three men, but Sholto <u>stole</u> the treasure. Small escaped with the help of <u>Tonga</u>, a native of the Andaman islands, who became his <u>accomplice</u>.

- Small and Tonga <u>tracked down</u> Sholto. Small was the man at Sholto's <u>window</u>, and he ransacked the room for <u>clues</u> about the treasure's location. When Bartholomew found the treasure, Tonga <u>killed</u> him and Small <u>took</u> the treasure.

- After Small finishes his story, Athelney Jones takes him to prison. Watson announces that he and Mary are <u>engaged</u>.

I deduce that Sherlock Holmes is a know-it-all...

For a fairly short novel, *The Sign of the Four* packs a lot in — treasure hunting, super-skilled dogs, lies, secrets and betrayal... Make sure you have the order of events and the characters sorted in your head before you turn the page.

Victorian Britain

The Sign of the Four was published in 1890, when steamboats, science and inequality were all the rage...

Britain changed dramatically in the Victorian era

> The Victorian era lasted from 1837 to 1901.

1) The novel is set in the <u>Victorian era</u>. The <u>main action</u> happens in <u>London</u> in <u>1888</u>, but much of the <u>backstory</u> takes place in <u>India</u> and <u>London</u> between the <u>1850s</u> and the <u>1880s</u>.

2) <u>Industry</u>, <u>science</u> and <u>technology</u> developed rapidly in the <u>Victorian era</u>. New <u>machines</u> were invented and lots of <u>factories</u> were built. <u>Steam power</u> was increasingly used in <u>industry</u> and <u>transport</u>.

3) London <u>expanded</u> rapidly in the <u>19th century</u>. Conan Doyle presents London as a <u>large</u>, <u>confusing</u> city where it's easy to get <u>lost</u>. Watson soon loses his "bearings" on the way to <u>Thaddeus's house</u> in Chapter Three because of his "<u>limited knowledge</u> of London".

> The <u>steamboat chase</u> in Chapter Ten would have seemed <u>thrilling</u> and <u>modern</u> to Victorian readers — Conan Doyle emphasises the <u>speed</u> of the <u>steamboats</u>, which go "flying" up the river "at a <u>tremendous rate</u>".

4) London's industries created <u>air pollution</u> and <u>smog</u>, which is reflected in Watson's descriptions of "<u>damp fog</u>" and "<u>steamy</u>" air.

The police began to use forensic science in their investigations

1) The 19th century saw the development of <u>forensic investigation</u> — this is the <u>examination</u> of <u>crime scenes</u> using <u>scientific methods</u>.

DEVELOPMENTS
- In the <u>1830s</u>, a scientist invented a <u>chemical test</u> that could <u>reveal</u> the presence of <u>arsenic</u> (a dangerous <u>poison</u>) in a person's body. Detectives used this test in <u>murder investigations</u>.
- <u>Pathologists</u> learned more about <u>human anatomy</u> by performing <u>autopsies</u> (examining dead bodies). In the late 19th century, the police could use <u>autopsies</u> to discover the <u>cause of death</u>.

> Holmes and Watson use their <u>knowledge</u> of the <u>effects of poison</u> to deduce that Bartholomew Sholto was <u>killed</u> with a "<u>strychnine-like substance</u>". Holmes visually <u>examines</u> the <u>body</u> to find out how the poison got into Bartholomew's <u>system</u>.

2) However, <u>forensic techniques</u> were still <u>limited</u>. Forensic analysis of <u>evidence</u> like hair, footprints and blood was <u>basic</u>, and <u>DNA analysis</u> wasn't invented until the <u>late 20th century</u>. This meant that it was still very <u>difficult</u> to <u>identify</u> criminals.

> Holmes's <u>forensic methods</u> are quite <u>advanced</u> for the time. In Chapter Six, he <u>analyses footprints</u>, which helps him to <u>identify</u> two suspects. Forensic scientists began to see the <u>value</u> of footprint evidence in the <u>1880s</u>, but it wasn't widely used by the police.

There was a lot of public interest in police investigations

1) <u>Newspapers</u> often kept the public <u>informed</u> on the <u>progress</u> of criminal investigations. Conan Doyle includes several <u>articles</u> about the police investigation into <u>Bartholomew Sholto's murder</u> in the novel.

2) The police were <u>criticised</u> by <u>newspapers</u> for failing to solve crimes, most notably during the <u>Jack the Ripper</u> case in <u>1888</u>, when detectives couldn't catch the <u>serial killer</u> who brutally <u>murdered</u> several women in London.

© Historical Images Archive / Alamy Stock Photo

> This <u>cartoon</u> was published in <u>1888</u> to <u>mock</u> London police. The policeman is looking for Jack the Ripper while <u>blindfolded</u> — it suggests the police are arresting suspects at <u>random</u> because they've <u>no idea</u> who the killer is.

3) The articles in the novel <u>praise</u> the police <u>excessively</u>, even though their investigation is <u>bad</u> — this humorously <u>underlines</u> their <u>incompetence</u>.

Victorian Britain

There was class division in Victorian Britain

1) The upper class (e.g. landowners) and middle class (e.g. doctors) lived comfortably. In contrast, the working class (e.g. factory workers) often had low incomes and struggled to survive. Many lived in slums, which were overcrowded and insanitary.

> Conan Doyle presents London as a city of extremes — there are "bediamonded women" at the theatre, but Watson also meets "dirty and ragged" street children.

2) Many upper and middle-class people looked down on the working classes. Holmes describes dock workers as "Dirty-looking rascals" — he judges the workers on their appearance, which shows that he feels superior to them.

Victorians often associated crime with the working class

- Many Victorians believed that there was a 'criminal class' made up of the poorest members of the working class. They thought that people from lower social classes were less moral than those from higher classes.
- The novel seems to challenge this association. Although the working-class character Jonathan Small commits immoral acts, he's also shown to be a victim of a middle-class criminal — Major Sholto.

3) People from different classes rarely mixed, and it was unusual for a person to marry someone from another social class. Watson, a middle-class man, thinks he won't be able to marry Mary once it is revealed she will inherit treasure. This wealth would enable her to move in higher social circles than Watson.

Men and women had different roles in Victorian society

1) Men and women occupied separate spheres:

WOMEN
- Women occupied the domestic sphere. They were expected to keep a comfortable home, be devoted to their family and obey their husband.
- Victorian women were meant to be gentle and passive. In the novel, the female characters wait at home while the men investigate the case.

> The ideal Victorian woman was known as 'The Angel in the House'. In the novel, Mary is described as "angelic" and Watson is comforted by the sight of Mary and Mrs Forrester when they are illuminated by light "shining through stained glass" as if they are in a church.

MEN
- Men worked outside the home in the public sphere to provide for their families. As a result, women often depended on men for financial security.
- Before marriage, men had to prove that they could support their bride. Watson worries his weak "banking-account" won't be enough for Mary.

2) Upper-class and middle-class women rarely worked, but there were 'respectable' jobs open to them — Mary works as a governess because her father is no longer there to support her financially.

3) Some women had enough money to support themselves. They were vulnerable to fortune-hunters — people who tried to improve their financial status by marrying someone rich. If she had inherited the treasure, Mary would have been a target for fortune-hunters.

> Watson worries he'll look like a "fortune-seeker" if he proposes to Mary. While many Victorian marriages were arranged with money in mind, obvious fortune-hunting was seen as improper.

Make sure you write about the novel's context in the exam...

Many of the themes in *The Sign of the Four* relate to the context of Victorian Britain. To get top marks, you need to be able to integrate comments about the novel's context, e.g. science and crime, into your answer.

© Heritage Image Partnership Ltd / Alamy Stock Photo

The British Empire and Colonisation

Some important parts of the novel's backstory are set in India between the 1850s and the 1880s.

Britain had an empire of overseas colonies

In the 19th century, Britain expanded its empire and established new colonies. It ruled these colonies and imposed its authority on them — this is called imperialism.

> A colony is a place that is ruled by another country and occupied by settlers from that country.

- The British army occupied many of its colonies to keep control of them. This is shown through the characters of Jonathan Small, Major Sholto and Captain Morstan, who are all in India with the British Indian army in the 1850s.
- The colonies were often treated as a source of wealth. To a modern audience, Major Sholto's theft of the treasure from India symbolises how Britain took valuable raw materials from its colonies and shipped them to Britain.
- Britain profited from cheap native labour, and slave labour was also used until slavery was abolished in the empire in 1838. In the novel, Small makes a "fair" living as a plantation "overseer" supervising Indian workers.

The Indian Rebellion of 1857 threatened British rule in India

1) In the 1850s, India was controlled by the East India Company, a powerful British trade organisation. It acted as an imperial power in India, collecting taxes and imposing laws. It profited from India's wealth.

2) The Company had a big private army made up of Indian soldiers (called sepoys) and British officers. In 1857, some sepoys staged a mutiny against the Company which sparked a wider revolt — the Indian Rebellion of 1857. This conflict was very bloody, and massacres were committed by both sides.

3) The rebellion was defeated in 1858. Control of India was transferred to the British Crown, and the East India Company lost its influence.

4) The rebellion divided Indian loyalties. In the novel, the Indian members of 'the four' supported the British. They felt entitled to the treasure because its owner, the rajah, had tried to be "friends" with both the sepoys and the British — they saw him as a traitor who had forfeited his right to the treasure.

> The rebellion shook British people's confidence in the empire. Its violent nature made people question the empire's security and increased fear of 'natives'.

The Victorians were prejudiced against foreign people

1) Victorians thought that British people were superior to native inhabitants of the colonies, who they called 'savages' because they viewed them as violent and uncivilised. They introduced the colonies' residents to British values to try to 'civilise' them so they were easier to govern. This is called cultural imperialism.

> Conan Doyle's presentation of Tonga, who is from the Andaman Islands, reflects these negative attitudes. Tonga is shown to be murderous, animalistic and amoral.

2) The Victorians increasingly feared the influence of foreign people. They worried that they might corrupt British culture. However, they were also fascinated by Indian culture.

> Mary wears a "small turban", and Thaddeus Sholto's home is full of Indian objects. He also has a loyal Indian "khitmutgar" (a male servant). This highlights his connection with India.

© Amoret Tanner / Alamy Stock Photo

KEY QUOTE

"there were two hundred thousand black devils let loose"

Conan Doyle's presentation of the rebellion is prejudiced and one-sided — Small's narrative portrays Indian soldiers as violent "devils", but British soldiers are presented as heroic saviours who bring "Peace".

Practice Questions

Now you've waded through the murky depths of Victorian history, it's time to have a go at some practice questions to check that everything's sunk in. The quick questions only need a short answer (a few words or a sentence should do it), but the in-depth questions are a bit more involved — try to write a paragraph of your best stuff for those ones. Have another look through the section if you're struggling with any of the answers.

Quick Questions

1) In which year do the main events of *The Sign of the Four* occur?

2) Name the two places where most of the novel's events take place.

3) Which of the following statements about Victorian London is NOT true?
   a) London grew larger during the Victorian period.
   b) London was changed by developments in steam power in the 19th century.
   c) The growth of industry had no negative effects on London.

4) Which of the following sentences is correct?
   a) Advanced forensic techniques were developed in the 19th century.
   b) Basic forensic techniques were developed in the 19th century.

5) Why did newspapers criticise London's police detectives in 1888?

6) Briefly explain why life might have been difficult for working-class Londoners.

7) Give one reason why people from higher classes looked down on working-class people.

8) Which 'sphere' were many women restricted to in the Victorian era?

9) Which event in India in the 1850s caused British people to worry about the British Empire?

10) Why did the Victorians sometimes refer to the native inhabitants of the colonies as 'savages'?

In-depth Questions

1) Do you think that Conan Doyle thought it was a good idea for detectives to use forensic techniques? Use evidence from the novel to explain your answer.

2) How are female characters portrayed in *The Sign of the Four*? What does this suggest about Victorian attitudes towards gender? Use quotes from the text in your answer.

3) What evidence is there in the novel that Victorians feared people from the colonies?

Analysis of Chapter One

The novel kicks off with a lengthy conversation between Sherlock Holmes and his lodger, Dr John Watson. Holmes amazes Watson by doing a fancy bit of deduction that makes him look really clever. Show off.

Holmes discusses his profession with Watson...

Theme — Friendship

This chapter introduces Holmes and Watson's friendship. Watson feels responsible for Holmes — he worries about his health and tries to persuade him that taking drugs is dangerous.

1) The novel opens with Holmes injecting cocaine, to Watson's disgust. Holmes explains that his mind "rebels at stagnation" and drugs stimulate his brain — he takes them when he doesn't have a case to work on.

2) Holmes thinks the "clarifying" effect that drugs have on his mind outweighs the negative physical effects. This shows he values his mind over his body.

3) Conan Doyle uses this chapter to introduce Holmes's profession and methods — he's a "consulting detective" who uses his "peculiar powers" to solve mysteries.

4) Holmes thinks that the "ideal detective" needs knowledge, and the skills of observation and deduction (reaching conclusions that are based on facts):

These techniques seem quite basic now, but they would have seemed ground-breaking to a 19th-century reader.

- Holmes is knowledgeable. He has written "several monographs" on "technical subjects", such as the nature of tobacco ash and the marks on a person's hands that reveal their occupation. This focus on "minutiae" (small details) emphasises his observation skills.

- Holmes carefully weighs up the evidence he has gathered through observation to make informed deductions.

... and demonstrates the art of deduction

1) Holmes deduces from Watson's appearance that Watson delivered a telegram that morning at a post office on Wigmore Street. This clever deduction proves the validity of Holmes's methods early in the novel.

2) Watson gives Holmes a "severe test" — he hands him a watch to analyse with "slight amusement" because he doesn't think that Holmes will succeed, but Holmes quickly makes some impressive deductions about Watson's brother, who previously owned the watch. This demonstrates Holmes's methods to the reader.

3) Holmes focuses on the "abstract problem" of the watch, forgetting that the subject of Watson's brother is "personal and painful" to Watson — this highlights his emotional coldness, which is a flaw in his character.

Mary Morstan's arrival changes the mood

1) After these brief demonstrations of his skill, Holmes reveals that a lack of "brain-work" makes him melancholy — this creates a sombre mood:

- He uses long sentences, slowing the pace and emphasising his boredom.
- His rhetorical questions suggest he views life without a case as pointless.

2) Mrs Hudson's (the housekeeper's) announcement of Mary Morstan's arrival changes the mood to one of anticipation:

- Holmes uses short sentences, suggesting that he is thinking rapidly.
- He uses commands, reflecting his newfound purposefulness.

© ITV/REX/Shutterstock

KEY QUOTE

"I abhor the dull routine of existence"

This chapter reveals a lot about Holmes's motives for pursuing strange and complicated cases. He finds ordinary life extremely boring, so he's always looking for a bit of "mental exaltation" to liven things up.

Analysis of Chapter Two

Things look up for Holmes in Chapter Two when Mary Morstan gives him an unusual case to get stuck into. Meanwhile, Watson falls in love with her and waits a whole hour before planning their future together.

Holmes and Watson meet Mary Morstan

1) Watson observes Mary carefully — he is immediately interested in her. He notices her "intense inward agitation" — this creates suspense because the reader must wait for the cause of her distress to be revealed.

2) She asks Holmes to help her to understand an "utterly inexplicable" situation — she offers him the mental stimulation that he desperately needs.

Character — Sherlock Holmes

Mary's employer recommended Holmes to Mary because of his "kindness and skill". He has a good reputation as a detective.

Mary introduces the novel's main mystery

1) Mary gives a concise, factual explanation of her case — her father, Captain Morstan, went missing in London ten years ago when he was on leave from the army in India. His friend, Major Sholto, was the only person in the city who knew Morstan, but he knew nothing about the disappearance.

Character — Sherlock Holmes

The prospect of a mystery changes Holmes — he becomes focused and enthusiastic. His eyes "glistened" — this contrasts with Chapter One, when they were "lack-lustre".

2) After replying six years ago to a newspaper advert asking for her address, Mary began to receive a "lustrous" pearl in the post each year.

When Holmes questions Mary about the letter, she gives him an answer that he "expected". This implies that he is holding back deductions he has already made, which increases the reader's anticipation.

3) The reason for Mary's visit is finally revealed — that morning, she received a letter telling her that she is a "wronged woman" and asking her to meet an unknown person at the Lyceum Theatre that evening. Holmes and Watson agree to accompany her.

Holmes and Watson have different reactions to Mary

1) Watson thinks that Mary is "very attractive", but Holmes doesn't "observe" this. Watson has a romantic interest in Mary, but Holmes only cares about her case. This highlights the difference in their characters.

2) Watson finds Holmes's lack of emotional interest in Mary "positively inhuman". However, Holmes believes that "emotional qualities" affect his ability to reason. He values this over making personal connections.

Background and Context

Watson's concerns reflect the fact that in the 19th century, men were expected to support their wives financially.

3) Holmes leaves to pursue the case — he is so eager to solve it that he acts immediately. Watson is distracted by thoughts of a romance with Mary, but worries his "weak leg and a weaker banking-account" might prevent it.

Write about how Conan Doyle uses dialogue...

Mary's conversation with Holmes and Watson reveals "the facts" of the case. Mention how Conan Doyle uses this dialogue to give the reader key information, which sets up the central mystery of the novel.

Analysis of Chapters Three and Four

Everything starts coming together nicely when Holmes brings home a "suggestive fact" (whatever that is), and Holmes, Watson and Mary head off on a coach trip into London's suburbs. No, not *that* kind of coach trip.

Holmes develops a theory about Major Sholto

1) Holmes <u>returns</u> to 221B Baker Street in "<u>excellent spirits</u>" after discovering that Mary received her <u>first pearl</u> less than a <u>week</u> after Major Sholto <u>died</u>.

2) He believes that Major Sholto's <u>heir</u> sent the <u>pearls</u> and the <u>letter</u> to Mary — he suggests that the heir wants to "make <u>compensation</u>" for something Major Sholto has done. It seems as though the case is coming together <u>easily</u>.

> **Character — Sherlock Holmes**
>
> Holmes is surprised when Watson <u>struggles</u> to see the <u>importance</u> of this connection. This shows that <u>making links</u> between facts comes much more <u>naturally</u> to Holmes.

There is a tense and eerie atmosphere in Chapter Three

1) Conan Doyle uses the <u>journey</u> to the <u>theatre</u> to build <u>suspense</u>:

   - Holmes takes a <u>gun</u>, which hints that there might be <u>danger</u> ahead.

   - Mary produces a "<u>curious paper</u>" that was found in her father's desk. It mentions "<u>The sign of the four</u>" and names Jonathan Small, Mahomet Singh, Abdullah Khan and Dost Akbar. Holmes asks Mary to "<u>Preserve</u> it". This suggests that it is <u>important</u>, but it's not clear <u>why</u>.

   - The setting creates a <u>gloomy</u>, <u>ominous</u> mood. "<u>Mud-coloured</u> clouds" hang "<u>sadly</u>" over the "<u>muddy</u>" streets, and the night is "<u>dull</u>" and "<u>heavy</u>".

   © ITV/REX/Shutterstock

2) The eerie mood makes Watson "<u>nervous</u> and <u>depressed</u>", but Holmes is above the "<u>petty influences</u>" of the <u>dreary</u> atmosphere and the <u>strangeness</u> of events. Nothing can <u>distract</u> him from the case.

3) From the theatre, a <u>coachman</u> takes them at a "<u>furious pace</u>" to a "<u>questionable</u>" area — this adds to the sense of <u>threat</u>. However, Holmes can <u>name</u> all the "<u>tortuous by-streets</u>" they take — he's <u>still in control</u>.

4) They are greeted by a <u>servant</u> at a "<u>dark</u>" house, and a <u>mysterious voice</u> calls to them from within. The reader has to wait to discover <u>who</u> the voice belongs to, which adds to the <u>suspense</u>.

Thaddeus Sholto reveals that Captain Morstan is dead

1) At the start of <u>Chapter Four</u>, Mary, Holmes and Watson meet <u>Thaddeus Sholto</u>, Major Sholto's son. He says that he can give Mary "<u>every information</u>" and that he can get her "<u>justice</u>". This suggests that Holmes's <u>theory</u> about Major Sholto's heir might be <u>true</u>.

2) Thaddeus <u>carelessly</u> mentions that Mary's father is <u>dead</u> — this resolves the <u>initial mystery</u> of why Captain Morstan <u>disappeared</u>. However, Thaddeus also introduces <u>more</u> mysteries:

   Major Sholto came back to England from <u>India</u> with "considerable" <u>wealth</u>. However, some "<u>mystery</u>" and "danger" hung over him — he was "very <u>fearful</u> of going out alone" and scared of <u>wooden-legged men</u>.

   <u>Six years ago</u>, the Major got a <u>letter</u> from India that gave him such a "<u>great shock</u>" that he "<u>sickened to</u> his <u>death</u>". Thaddeus and his brother, Bartholomew, <u>never found out</u> what was in the letter.

KEY QUOTE

"We were driving to an unknown place, on an unknown errand"

Watson's repetition of "unknown" hammers home just how mysterious their quest is — they've no idea where they're going or why. It's lucky that he's got Sherlock 'London A to Z' Holmes to distract him, really.

Analysis of Chapter Four (continued)

Chapter Four is mostly just Watson telling a story about Thaddeus Sholto telling a story about Major Sholto telling a story about himself. Complicated? I don't know what you mean...

Major Sholto felt guilty about his actions

© Chris Wooley

1) In his father's "own very words", Thaddeus tells the Major's story:

- The Major and Captain Morstan acquired a "considerable treasure" in India. They argued over how to share it, and Morstan collapsed and died.

- Fearing that he would be blamed for Morstan's death, Sholto hid the body and took Morstan's share of the treasure for himself.

2) The Major asked his sons to give Mary a "fair share" of the treasure. He realised that he had wrongly kept the treasure out of greed, which makes the reader more sympathetic towards him.

3) Major Sholto was about to reveal the treasure's location when he became frantic with terror after seeing a man with "wild cruel eyes" at the window. The shock of this killed the Major.

4) The next morning, the brothers discovered that Major Sholto's room had been ransacked and a note had appeared on the Major's chest with "The sign of the four" written on it. This suggests that the Major is linked to the paper from Captain Morstan's desk, which deepens the mystery.

Writer's Techniques — Narrative

Major Sholto's story is reported third hand (through Thaddeus and Watson). This makes it less reliable, as the chance that one of the narrators is misremembering is higher.

> Holmes and Watson aren't present when the Major dies, but it reminds the reader that they are involved in something dangerous.

Thaddeus's story resolves parts of the mystery

1) The brothers searched the family home (Pondicherry Lodge) for the treasure, but they couldn't find it.

2) However, the mystery of the pearls is solved:

Thaddeus explains that he convinced Bartholomew to let him send Mary a pearl at "fixed intervals". He wanted to stop her becoming "destitute", but Bartholomew didn't want to give away any of the pearls. Thaddeus claims that Bartholomew has their "father's fault" (greed).

Character — Thaddeus Sholto

The "difference of opinion" between the brothers caused Thaddeus to move out of Pondicherry Lodge. He was prepared to sacrifice his home for his principles, which shows he is moral and strong-willed.

3) After he has finished his story, Thaddeus reveals that the treasure has finally been discovered hidden in the ceiling at Pondicherry Lodge — delaying this revelation increases its impact on the reader.

KEY EVENT

Writer's Techniques — Language

Watson uses figurative language to describe "selfishness" taking him "by the soul" and his heart feeling "as heavy as lead" — this reinforces his emotional nature.

4) Thaddeus takes everyone to Pondicherry Lodge to demand Mary's share of the treasure. He is determined to get justice for Mary.

5) On the journey, Thaddeus reveals that the Agra treasure is worth at least "half a million" sterling. Watson is "downcast" at this news — he thinks Mary won't be interested in him if she's wealthy.

EXAM TIP

Comment on Conan Doyle's use of embedded narratives...

In the exam, you could write about how Thaddeus's narrative gives the reader an insight into a character who is already dead — Major Sholto. Thaddeus claims to be repeating exactly what his father told him.

Analysis of Chapter Five

Holmes and Co. get a nasty surprise when they arrive at Pondicherry Lodge to meet Brother Bartholomew, who is actually Thaddeus's brother, Bartholomew. See, this is why we need commas.

Everyone arrives at Pondicherry Lodge

1) Pondicherry Lodge is like a <u>fortress</u> — the grounds are surrounded by "high" walls topped with "<u>broken glass</u>", and there is only <u>one</u> "iron-clamped" <u>entrance</u>. This makes the house seem <u>unwelcoming</u> and emphasises that it conceals secrets (see p.54).

2) The gatekeeper <u>refuses</u> to let them in at first, but he is very <u>friendly</u> once Holmes <u>reminds</u> him that they've <u>boxed</u> together. This shows that Holmes has numerous <u>talents</u> and can <u>fit in</u> with <u>different types</u> of people.

3) The grounds are "<u>desolate</u>", and the house is "plunged in <u>shadow</u>" and "<u>deathly silence</u>". This creates an <u>unsettling</u> mood.

Theme — Love

Mary and John's <u>romance</u> develops in this chapter. They "<u>instinctively</u>" hold hands when they're <u>scared</u>, showing their <u>natural attraction</u>. They take <u>stereotypical</u> gender roles, with Mary seeking Watson's "<u>protection</u>".

Conan Doyle gradually builds suspense in this chapter

The <u>housekeeper</u> reveals that Bartholomew is <u>locked</u> in his room with "<u>such a face</u> on him", but she doesn't give <u>details</u>. Her fear hints that something <u>bad</u> has happened.	Holmes <u>leads</u> the way upstairs to Bartholomew's room very <u>slowly</u>, stopping to examine "mere <u>shapeless smudges</u>". This <u>delays</u> their arrival at the room.	Holmes looks through the <u>keyhole</u> into the room and "<u>instantly</u>" looks away. This builds tension as the reader <u>doesn't know</u> what he's <u>seen</u> to cause this <u>reaction</u>.

The suspense is <u>resolved</u> when Watson looks through the keyhole and sees Bartholomew's <u>body</u>, but his initial belief that it is <u>Thaddeus</u> adds <u>horror</u> and makes the mystery seem <u>supernatural</u>.

The case becomes even more mysterious

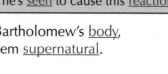

1) Inside the room, Holmes inspects the crime scene and <u>deduces</u> that Bartholomew has been <u>murdered</u>, but the <u>circumstances</u> are <u>strange</u>:

Writer's Techniques

Conan Doyle holds back <u>some</u> deductions to create <u>anticipation</u>. Holmes says that he almost has a "<u>connected</u> case", but he <u>doesn't explain</u> the links. This keeps the reader in <u>suspense</u>.

- The <u>door</u> of the room was "locked on the <u>inside</u>" when Holmes and Watson arrived. It's not clear <u>how</u> Bartholomew's <u>killer</u> could have <u>left</u> the room, which makes the <u>mystery</u> seem impossible to <u>solve</u>.

- There is a <u>note</u> near the body with "The sign of the four" on it, like the one that was found on <u>Major Sholto's</u> body. This suggests that the two deaths are <u>linked</u>, and adds to the sense of <u>fear</u> by hinting that there could be <u>more</u> murders.

- Holmes <u>quickly</u> uncovers the <u>cause</u> of Bartholomew's death — a "<u>poisoned</u>" thorn. This <u>unusual</u> murder weapon adds to the <u>mystery</u>.

2) Conan Doyle adds another <u>layer</u> of <u>mystery</u> at the <u>end</u> of the chapter — Bartholomew has been "<u>robbed</u>" of the <u>treasure</u>. This builds <u>excitement</u> — just as the treasure seems to be <u>within reach</u>, it is <u>lost</u> again.

"There is something devilish in this, Watson"

Holmes's reaction when he sees Bartholomew's body suggests that he wasn't expecting the case to take this sinister turn. This makes the case seem more scary, as even level-headed Holmes is shocked by it.

Analysis of Chapter Six

There's some comic relief in this chapter when Mr Athelney Jones turns up and starts to make a fool of himself. Holmes soon calls for backup from his friend Toby, the best canine detective in London. Aww...

Holmes examines the crime scene methodically

1) Thaddeus has left to fetch the <u>police</u>, and Holmes talks Watson through his <u>deductions</u>.

- Holmes's speech is full of <u>concise</u> and <u>factual</u> observations — this <u>increases</u> the <u>pace</u> of his <u>dialogue</u>, which shows how <u>quickly</u> his mind <u>jumps</u> from one observation to another.
- Holmes encourages Watson to think <u>logically</u>. He presents the <u>facts</u> for him and invites him to make a <u>deduction</u>. This gives the reader some <u>insight</u> into the way that Holmes <u>thinks</u>.

2) Holmes identifies <u>two perpetrators</u> — a man with a <u>wooden leg</u> who entered the <u>locked room</u> through the <u>window</u>, and an "<u>ally</u>" who <u>entered</u> through a <u>trapdoor</u> in the <u>roof</u> of the room <u>above</u>.

3) In this room, they discover <u>footprints</u> that are "<u>half the size</u>" of an ordinary <u>man's</u>. Watson wonders if they belong to a <u>child</u>. This is the <u>most obvious</u> deduction, but Holmes <u>dismisses</u> it — he doesn't <u>jump to conclusions</u>.

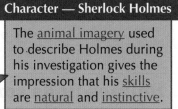

Character — Sherlock Holmes

The <u>animal imagery</u> used to describe Holmes during his investigation gives the impression that his <u>skills</u> are <u>natural</u> and <u>instinctive</u>.

4) Holmes <u>searches</u> for clues with "beady eyes" like a "<u>bird</u>" — he's <u>very aware</u> of his surroundings. He <u>moves</u> like a "<u>blood-hound</u>", as though he's a skilled <u>hunter</u>. This suggests that the <u>murderer</u> won't escape <u>easily</u>.

5) Holmes <u>encourages</u> Watson to observe that the <u>poisoned thorn</u> used to kill Bartholomew isn't "<u>English</u>". This hints that the murderer is <u>foreign</u>, which plays to <u>Victorian racial prejudices</u>.

Athelney Jones arrests Thaddeus for murder

© Chris Wooley

1) The arrival of the police <u>disrupts</u> Holmes's <u>methodical</u> investigation. Athelney Jones starts to <u>theorise wildly</u>, weaving a "<u>web</u>" around Thaddeus. He tries to make the <u>facts</u> fit his <u>theory</u>, instead of looking at the <u>evidence</u>.

2) Jones <u>arrests</u> Thaddeus, even though Holmes <u>shows</u> him the evidence that he's <u>missed</u>. This makes Jones look <u>incompetent</u>. Holmes proves his <u>superior skill</u> by telling Jones who he thinks <u>really</u> committed the <u>murder</u>:

- He names the <u>wooden-legged</u> man as <u>Jonathan Small</u>. This makes Holmes look <u>brilliant</u>, as he makes this <u>precise</u> deduction with little <u>evidence</u>.
- He gives a <u>detailed description</u> of Small and introduces a <u>new theory</u> — Small is a "<u>convict</u>". It seems like he's <u>close</u> to <u>solving</u> the case.

3) The <u>mystery</u> isn't <u>fully resolved</u> as Small's <u>ally</u> hasn't been <u>identified</u> yet. This keeps the reader <u>interested</u> and helps the plot <u>keep</u> its <u>momentum</u>.

Theme — Duality

<u>Holmes</u> and <u>Jones</u> <u>contrast</u> — they have very <u>different approaches</u> to detective work.

4) Holmes asks Watson to fetch <u>Toby the dog</u>, who has an "amazing <u>power</u> of <u>scent</u>", to follow a trail of <u>creosote</u> (a type of oil) that Small's accomplice trod in. Holmes would rather have Toby than "the <u>whole detective force</u> of London" — this would have <u>amused</u> Victorian readers as it emphasises the <u>inadequacy</u> of the police (see p.6).

KEY QUOTE

"whatever remains, however improbable, must be the truth"

Holmes's deductions may sometimes be hard to believe, but they're always based on all the facts. He's all about getting to the truth, so he comes up with theories that account for all the evidence.

Analysis of Chapter Seven

While Athelney Jones continues to arrest anything with a pulse, Holmes and Watson hunt for the real killers.

Watson hides his feelings for Mary

1) Watson takes Mary <u>home</u>. His <u>feelings</u> for her have <u>intensified</u>, but he <u>doesn't confess</u> them to her for <u>two main reasons</u>:

- He thinks it's wrong to <u>force</u> "words of <u>affection</u>" on her when she's in a "<u>weak</u> and <u>helpless</u>" state. This shows he's <u>honourable</u>.
- He worries that Mary will think he is a "vulgar <u>fortune-seeker</u>" — he doesn't want her to think he is interested in her <u>money</u>. Having Mary's <u>good opinion</u> means more to him than his own <u>happiness</u>.

2) Conan Doyle hints that Watson and Mary will <u>overcome</u> these setbacks. Watson says that Mary has "<u>since</u>" told him that she thought he was "<u>cold</u> and <u>distant</u>" on this journey. This suggests that their relationship becomes <u>closer</u> than it is at this point.

© ITV/REX/Shutterstock

Background and Context

In the 19th century, <u>wealth</u> brought <u>power</u>. This meant that an <u>heiress</u> may have been the <u>target</u> of men wanting to increase their own wealth and status.

Holmes finds some more evidence

Writer's Techniques — Irony

Holmes says that Jones showed an "<u>immense display of energy</u>" in making the arrests, but the reader knows he has arrested the <u>wrong</u> people — this creates <u>irony</u>.

1) Watson returns to <u>Pondicherry Lodge</u> with Toby and learns that Jones has <u>arrested</u> the household staff. This makes Jones's approach seem <u>irrational</u>.

2) In contrast, Holmes is calm and ready to look for <u>more clues</u>. He points out the <u>trail of creosote</u> and goes on to the <u>roof</u> to follow it to the <u>ground</u>.

3) On the roof, he finds a "<u>pouch</u>" of <u>thorns</u> like the one used to <u>kill</u> Bartholomew. It's made from <u>exotic</u> materials like "coloured <u>grasses</u>" — this supports Holmes's theory that <u>Small's associate</u> is <u>foreign</u>.

Toby tries to track down Small's associate

1) Holmes explains his <u>theories</u> about <u>Jonathan Small</u> to Watson as they <u>follow</u> Toby, who is "eagerly" <u>pursuing</u> the creosote trail. This fills in some <u>gaps</u> in the case without <u>slowing</u> the <u>pace</u> of the novel.

- Holmes thinks that Small drew a <u>map</u> to the treasure for <u>Major Sholto</u> and <u>Captain Morstan</u>. Small couldn't get the treasure <u>himself</u> because he was imprisoned. The officers <u>betrayed</u> Small and <u>took</u> the treasure.
- Small <u>escaped</u> and went to get <u>revenge</u> on Major Sholto — he was the man who appeared at the Major's <u>window</u>. After the Major's death, Small searched his room for the treasure and left the 'sign of the four' note.
- He kept a "<u>secret watch</u>" on the Major's sons, so he knew when they found the treasure. Small's <u>associate</u> helped him get into the room, but <u>accidentally</u> trod in <u>creosote</u>. The associate <u>killed</u> Bartholomew.

2) Holmes loads his <u>gun</u>, which hints that there's <u>danger</u> ahead — this creates <u>tension</u>. However, Toby then follows the <u>wrong trail</u>. This <u>unexpected twist</u> creates <u>humour</u> and breaks the <u>tension</u>.

Watson sees the case as a "<u>labyrinth</u>" — solving <u>one mystery</u> introduces a "<u>deeper</u>" one. It seems <u>impossible</u> to solve, which makes Holmes's <u>progress remarkable</u>.

EXAM TIP

You could write about Conan Doyle's use of suspense...

Conan Doyle ramps up the suspense by implying that Toby is closing in on his target, but this suspense is quickly shattered when Watson and Holmes break into a massive laughing fit at the end of the chapter.

Analysis of Chapter Eight

Things start to look promising when Toby gets back on the scent, but the trail soon goes cold again.

Holmes learns that Small escaped on the Aurora

1) Toby quickly finds the right trail, which leads to Mordecai Smith's wharf on the River Thames.

2) Smith's wife explains that her husband left on the Aurora (his steam boat) the previous morning with their son and a "wooden-legged man". This confirms that Small has escaped.

> A wharf is a landing platform where boats can load and unload.

3) Holmes pretends he wants to hire the Aurora — he knows that Mrs Smith is more likely to talk to a potential customer. He asks a series of clever questions to build up a detailed description of the boat.

Character — Sherlock Holmes

Holmes uses his intelligence to manipulate others. He is able to make people give away information that they would normally protect.

> The Smith family are from a lower social class than Holmes. He describes them as "people of that sort". His dismissive and patronising tone suggests that he feels superior to them.

> See p.7 for more about class.

The Baker Street irregulars set off to find the Aurora

1) Holmes pays his "unofficial force", a gang of street children, to look for the Aurora, because they can "go everywhere" and "see everything". Holmes's unconventional methods make him seem inventive.

> The children "buzzed" down the stairs and went "streaming" along the street. Their energy suggests that they'll be an effective tool.

2) Handing over the search for the Aurora pauses Holmes and Watson's activities. Holmes stays active by researching Small's accomplice's background, whereas Watson is content to rest and think about Mary.

Theme — Love

> The strength of Watson's love for Mary becomes clear in this chapter. He is ready to "devote" his life to finding the treasure because it is "rightfully" hers, even though he believes that finding it will put her "forever beyond" his reach. This shows his feelings to be selfless and honourable.

© ITV/REX/Shutterstock

Holmes reveals the identity of Small's ally

Background and Context

In the 19th century, many British people thought that people from the colonies of the British Empire were uncivilised. Watson refers to Small's associate as a "savage".

1) Holmes explains his theory that Small's accomplice is from the Andaman Islands near India. He reads from a book that's full of stereotypical Victorian ideas — it claims Andaman natives are cannibals who commit "massacres". It stresses their brutality and makes them sound inhuman by referring to their "distorted features" and "misshapen heads".

2) Conan Doyle has previously kept the reader in suspense by hinting at the man's identity. Rather than breaking the tension, revealing details about him now makes him seem more mysterious and frightening.

3) Holmes thinks that things would have been more "ghastly" if Small hadn't controlled his ally. This shifts blame onto the ally, reflecting the view that people from other countries were more violent than Britons.

KEY QUOTE

"he began to play some low, dreamy, melodious air"

At the end of the chapter, Holmes improvises a "soft" violin piece to help Watson fall asleep "peacefully". This shows that Holmes is not as emotionally detached as he claims to be, as he clearly cares for Watson.

Analysis of Chapter Nine

The investigation stalls a bit when the Aurora is nowhere to be found. Watson stays at 221B while Holmes disguises himself as a crotchety old sailor and heads off to the Thames to try and reel in some fresh leads.

The case begins to frustrate Holmes

1) The Aurora is still <u>missing</u> — Holmes is "<u>surprised</u> and <u>disappointed</u>" that there are no new clues.

2) <u>Watson</u> goes to <u>update</u> Mary on the case. He feels a "<u>thrill of joy</u>" when Mary only shows "<u>small interest</u>" in the treasure. Watson's <u>preoccupation</u> with Mary contrasts with Holmes's <u>fixation</u> on the case.

3) Conan Doyle emphasises Holmes's <u>agitation</u> in this chapter:

> • Mrs Hudson hears him <u>pacing</u> in his room and "<u>muttering</u>" to himself.
>
> • He describes the case as an "<u>infernal problem</u>" that is "<u>consuming</u>" him — he finds it <u>maddening</u> that he can't make <u>progress</u>.
>
> • He tries to <u>occupy</u> his <u>mind</u> with <u>science</u> — he does some complicated "<u>chemical analysis</u>" late into the night, which suggests that he can't <u>settle</u>.

Character — Sherlock Holmes

This lack of progress makes Holmes "<u>dejected</u>" and "<u>morose</u>". He quickly becomes <u>depressed</u>, as he was in Chapter One before the investigation. This shows how <u>closely</u> Holmes's <u>mental wellbeing</u> is linked to solving cases.

4) Holmes's <u>frustration</u> causes him to pursue the Aurora <u>himself</u> — he wants to <u>regain control</u> of the case.

Watson briefly doubts Holmes's methods

1) Watson wonders whether Holmes looks for "<u>subtle</u>", "<u>bizarre</u>" explanations when "<u>plainer</u>" ones exist. This makes the reader <u>question</u> Holmes's <u>theories</u>, which adds <u>tension</u> because he offers the <u>only hope</u> of solving the case.

2) <u>Athelney Jones</u> arrives. He is "<u>meek</u>" and "<u>apologetic</u>", and he acknowledges Holmes's <u>superior skill</u>. This makes Watson's doubts seem <u>unfounded</u>.

3) Jones produces a <u>telegram</u> from <u>Holmes</u> that says he is "<u>close</u> on the track of the <u>Sholto gang</u>". This <u>restores</u> the reader's <u>confidence</u> in Holmes.

Writer's Techniques — Narrative

Conan Doyle uses a <u>telegram</u>, a <u>news article</u> and an <u>advert</u> to tell the story while Watson <u>waits</u> for Holmes to return. These reveal <u>details</u> such as the <u>release</u> of Thaddeus Sholto.

Holmes is on the trail of the criminals

1) An old man in "<u>seafaring garb</u>" comes to Baker Street. The man is Holmes in <u>disguise</u>. Watson is <u>fooled</u>, so the <u>reader</u> is also <u>tricked</u> — there is <u>no reason</u> to <u>doubt</u> Watson's <u>description</u> of the man.

2) Holmes has been "<u>working</u>" in disguise because the "<u>criminal classes</u>" can <u>recognise</u> him by sight. This suggests that he has a <u>reputation</u> among <u>criminals</u> as well as those who want to <u>hire</u> him.

> <u>Undercover police work</u> was still quite <u>new</u> in the late 19th century, so Holmes's idea of using a <u>disguise</u> would have seemed quite <u>innovative</u>.

© Chris Wooley

3) Holmes says that Jones can take the "<u>official credit</u>" for catching Small if he follows Holmes's <u>orders</u>. He uses Jones's <u>vanity</u> to get what he needs — he immediately asks for a fast <u>police boat</u>.

EXAM TIP

Make sure you comment on the novel's context...

You could write about how the character of Jones reflects the public's perception of the police at the time as bungling and inept — even a modern reader may find the way his authority is undermined entertaining.

Analysis of Chapters Ten and Eleven

Events reach a climax when Holmes and Watson take part in an epic steamboat chase on the River Thames.

Conan Doyle builds the momentum in Chapter Ten

1) At the start of Chapter Ten, Holmes is in a "state of nervous exaltation". This suggests that something exciting and important is going to happen in this chapter, which heightens the reader's anticipation.

2) Conan Doyle increases the suspense by hinting that there will be a high-speed steamboat chase — Holmes, Watson and Jones board a "very fast" police boat, and the Aurora is also known for its speed.

3) The chase seems imminent. While undercover, Holmes found the Aurora at Jacobson's boatyard and learned that Small and his associate would be leaving on it at "eight o'clock sharp". It is "a little past seven" when Holmes and the others get to their boat, so it's likely the pursuit will happen soon.

The steamboat chase creates an exciting atmosphere

When the Aurora has been sighted and the chase begins, Conan Doyle creates a sense of urgency and excitement:

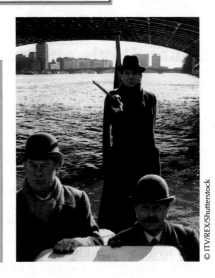

- Short sentences and exclamations, like "Heap it on, stokers!", add pace.

- The Aurora "thundered on" and the police boat's engines are described as a "great metallic heart". This highlights the power and speed of the boats, which creates a sense of energy and makes the chase thrilling.

- The description of Small's associate adds horror and danger to the chase. He is referred to as a "distorted creature" who is "marked with all bestiality and cruelty". This makes him seem unnatural and monstrous.

- The danger increases at the climax of the chase — Small's ally fires a dart at the police boat and is shot and killed by Watson and Holmes. It seems like Small might escape when he jumps ashore, but his wooden leg gets stuck and he is captured. This ends the sense of threat.

© ITV/REX/Shutterstock

Small is caught, but the treasure has gone

1) Chapter Eleven opens with a description of Small. The reader expects an unpleasant and violent criminal, but Small shows "more sorrow than anger" and has a "gleam of something like humour in his eyes". This humanises him and encourages the reader to feel sympathy for him.

2) This sympathy is strengthened when Small speaks. He says that his ally, Tonga, murdered Bartholomew, which Small feels "grieved" about — he had "no quarrel" with Bartholomew. He confesses that he would have killed Major Sholto, hinting that he was wronged by the Major.

> Small is presented as a victim as well as a criminal, making him more complex. In contrast, Tonga is portrayed as senselessly savage.

3) Watson takes the treasure chest to Mary with a "heavy" heart — he thinks he will lose her.

4) However, the box is empty. This is a turning point in Mary and Watson's relationship. The treasure is no longer a "barrier" between them, so Watson is free to confess his love.

KEY EVENT

EXAM TIP

Don't forget to discuss the novel's themes...

Small describes the Agra treasure as a "curse" that has brought only "murder", "fear", "guilt", and "slavery" to the people who have tried to possess it — you could link this to the negative consequences of greed.

Analysis of Chapter Twelve

Most of the final chapter is about Small's past and his link to the treasure — he weaves a rip-roaring tale of treasure-hunting, betrayal and murder that fills in all the blanks for Holmes, Watson and Jones. Handy.

The characters discuss justice

1) Small threw the treasure into the <u>river</u> to stop <u>Sholto's</u> and <u>Morstan's</u> "kin" from <u>getting</u> it. He doesn't think they have "<u>any right</u>" to the treasure.

2) Jones accuses Small of "<u>thwarting</u>" justice by throwing away the treasure, but Small thinks that it would be an <u>injustice</u> if it went to those who hadn't "<u>earned</u> it". Small believes that he deserves the treasure because he spent "<u>Twenty long years</u>" as a <u>convict</u> for it.

> **Theme — Justice**
> This contrast highlights the <u>message</u> that people can have very <u>different ideas</u> about the nature of <u>justice</u>.

3) To work out "<u>how far justice</u>" was on Small's side, Holmes asks Small to tell <u>his story</u>. He wants all the <u>facts</u>, showing he is <u>fair</u> and <u>non-judgemental</u>.

© Chris Wooley

Conan Doyle encourages the reader to feel sympathy for Small

1) Small outlines his difficult <u>past</u>. He joined the <u>army</u> as a young man, but while in <u>India</u>, his leg was bitten off by a <u>crocodile</u>. This <u>ended</u> his army career and made him feel like a "<u>useless cripple</u>". This increases the reader's <u>sympathy</u> for him.

> See p.8 for more on the British Empire.

2) He found work on a <u>plantation</u> overseeing <u>labourers</u> and was "<u>content</u>", but says that India became a "<u>perfect hell</u>" when the "<u>great mutiny</u>" broke out. This makes him seem <u>unlucky</u>.

3) Small presents himself as a <u>victim</u> of <u>violence</u>. He describes the <u>Indians</u> who took part in the revolt as "<u>black fiends</u>" who <u>shot</u> at him and <u>brutally murdered</u> people he knew.

> **Writer's Techniques — Narrative**
> Small is an <u>unreliable narrator</u>. He only tells <u>his side</u> of the story, so the reader doesn't get a <u>balanced view</u>.

> **Background and Context**
> The "great mutiny" refers to the <u>Indian Rebellion of 1857</u>. This was a military revolt which began when a group of sepoys (<u>Indian soldiers</u> in the British Indian army) <u>rebelled</u> against British rule (see p.8).

Small explains how 'the four' came together

1) Small <u>fled</u> to the British <u>fort</u> at Agra, where he joined a <u>volunteer group</u> fighting the rebels. He was put in <u>command</u> of <u>two Sikhs</u> who would become members of '<u>the four</u>' — Mahomet Singh and Abdullah Khan.

> Sikhs are followers of Sikhism, one of India's major religions. Many Sikhs served in the British Indian army in the 19th century.

2) The Sikhs gave Small an <u>ultimatum</u> — he could either help them <u>kill</u> a man for his <u>treasure</u> or they would <u>kill Small</u>. Small portrays himself as a <u>victim</u> — he makes it seems like he had <u>no choice</u> but to help them.

3) Achmet (the carrier of the treasure) came to Agra with <u>Dost Akbar</u>, the fourth member of '<u>the four</u>', and was <u>murdered</u> by them. They <u>hid</u> the treasure and drew up four <u>plans</u> showing its <u>location</u>.

4) The <u>events</u> in Small's story suggest that he is <u>not</u> completely <u>immoral</u>:

   - He made sure the <u>fort</u> would not be "<u>endangered</u>" before he agreed to help the Sikhs. This makes him seem <u>selfless</u> and <u>patriotic</u>, as he valued the <u>safety of Agra</u> over his own <u>life</u> and the <u>treasure</u>.

   - Small <u>swore an oath</u> that he would always be loyal to 'the four'. He's <u>kept</u> this <u>promise</u>, which shows that he's <u>trustworthy</u>.

> **Character — Jonathan Small**
> Small is still largely presented as an <u>unpleasant</u> character. Watson reacts to him with "<u>utmost horror</u>", and Holmes and Jones show "<u>disgust</u>" after hearing his story.

Analysis of Chapter Twelve

Small reveals that Major Sholto betrayed 'the four'

1) The four men were <u>arrested</u> for <u>Achmet's murder</u> and sent to a <u>convict colony</u> on the <u>Andaman Islands</u>, where Major Sholto and Captain Morstan were stationed.

2) Small "<u>behaved well</u>" and got some <u>privileges</u> — this seems to have been with a view to escaping, which shows his <u>cunning</u>. He <u>manipulated</u> the officers to try to secure his <u>freedom</u>:

Convict colonies were remote settlements where prisoners lived and worked under the supervision of British officials.

- Small knew that <u>Major Sholto</u> had <u>lost</u> all of his <u>money</u> playing cards and was a "<u>ruined man</u>". He realised that Sholto would be <u>vulnerable</u> to <u>bribery</u>.
- He told Sholto about the "<u>hidden treasure</u>" and suggested a <u>bargain</u> — Sholto and his friend Morstan would get a <u>share</u> of the treasure if they helped 'the four' <u>escape</u>.

KEY EVENT

3) The plan <u>failed</u> because of Sholto's <u>greed</u>. Sholto, Morstan and 'the four' swore "<u>solemn oaths</u>", but Sholto <u>betrayed</u> them and took <u>all</u> the treasure <u>without freeing</u> 'the four'.

4) From this point onward, Small was driven by his "<u>overpowering</u>, absorbing passion" for <u>revenge</u> on Sholto — it drove his <u>escape</u>, his <u>pursuit</u> of Sholto and his <u>theft</u> of the treasure from Pondicherry Lodge. He was ready to risk the "<u>gallows</u>" for revenge, showing that this desire was more <u>powerful</u> than his fear of the <u>law</u>.

The rest of the mystery is resolved

1) Small gives more detail about his <u>accomplice</u> — an "<u>Andaman Islander</u>" named <u>Tonga</u>, who he <u>nursed</u> to health. This shows Small's <u>caring side</u>.

2) Small knows that Tonga was "<u>devoted</u>" to him and "would do <u>anything</u>" for him, but he <u>used</u> Tonga — first to help him <u>escape</u>, then by "<u>exhibiting</u>" him at fairs for <u>money</u>, then to help him <u>steal</u> the treasure. This suggests that he <u>didn't really care</u> about Tonga.

Theme — Imperialism

Small's treatment of Tonga symbolises the way that British people <u>exploited</u> India's <u>people</u> and <u>resources</u> in the 19th century.

Character — Sherlock Holmes

Holmes shows an <u>interest</u> in tiny details, such as Small bringing his own rope to Pondicherry Lodge — this shows his need to understand <u>every</u> aspect of the case.

3) Small explains that he left the 'sign of the four' <u>notes</u> as a sign that <u>justice</u> had been done — the treasure had gone back to those "<u>who had most right</u>" to it. The notes were a vital <u>clue</u> in helping Holmes catch Small, suggesting that Small's <u>distorted</u> idea of justice brought about his <u>downfall</u>.

The novel has a bittersweet ending

1) The ending is <u>satisfying</u> for the reader. The <u>mystery</u> is <u>solved</u> and the '<u>criminal</u>' has been <u>caught</u>. However, Holmes goes back to his "<u>cocaine-bottle</u>" — the case has only given him <u>temporary</u> relief.

2) Watson announces his <u>engagement to Mary</u>. This is a <u>happy event</u>, but it is tinged with <u>sadness</u> because Watson thinks it will stop him from <u>spending time</u> with Holmes and "<u>studying</u>" his methods.

© Chris Wooley

KEY QUOTE

"It's been the sign of four with us always."

This chapter reveals that Small is not quite as evil as the reader may have expected. His immoral actions are often motivated by his sense of justice (which we may or may not agree with) and loyalty to 'the four'.

Practice Questions

There's a lot going on in 'The Sign of the Four', so it's a good idea to get the plot straight in your head. Have a go at these questions to check you've mastered it all. Remember, you don't need to write loads — a few sentences for each quick question and a paragraph for each in-depth question will do nicely.

Quick Questions

1) Briefly explain why Holmes takes drugs.

2) Give two mysteries that Mary introduces in Chapter Two.

3) Why does Thaddeus Sholto want to help Mary?

4) What is unusual about the weapon that is used to kill Bartholomew?

5) How does Conan Doyle make Athelney Jones appear incompetent?

6) In Chapter Seven, why doesn't Watson tell Mary how he feels?

7) In your own words, outline why Holmes asks the Baker Street irregulars to search for the Aurora, rather than going himself.

8) How does Holmes advance the investigation in Chapter Nine when there are no new leads?

9) Why does Small throw the Agra treasure into the Thames?

10) Explain why Small wanted to get revenge on Major Sholto.

In-depth Questions

1) When Holmes makes deductions about Watson's brother in Chapter One, he says "I could only say what was the balance of probability. I did not at all expect to be so accurate."

   Do you think Holmes really is surprised that his deductions were so accurate?
   Use evidence from Chapter One to help you explain your answer.

2) Why do you think Conan Doyle includes the character of Athelney Jones in the novel?

3) When Holmes finds the Aurora at Jacobson's Yard, Watson isn't with him. Why do you think Conan Doyle chose to separate them at this point in the plot? Explain your answer.

4) The novel ends with Holmes and Watson talking about the case and the future.
   Why do you think Conan Doyle ended the novel in this way? Explain your answer.

Practice Questions

Now you've got your brain nice and warm, it's time to have a go at some exam-style questions. I know, it's not exactly what you wanted to read, but these practice questions will really help you to nail your essay-writing skills. Don't take them all on at once — pick one that you like the look of and give it a good go under exam conditions. You don't need to write a full essay for all of them — just coming up with a good plan can be useful.

Exam-style Questions

1) Read this extract from Chapter One, then answer the question below.

> "I am the last and highest court of appeal in detection. When Gregson or Lestrade or Athelney Jones are out of their depths — which, by the way, is their normal state — the matter is laid before me. I examine the data, as an expert, and pronounce a specialist's opinion. I claim no credit in such cases. My name figures in no newspaper. The work itself, the pleasure of finding a field for my peculiar powers, is my highest reward. But you have yourself had some experience of my methods of work in the Jefferson Hope case."
>
> "Yes, indeed," said I, cordially. "I was never so struck by anything in my life. I even embodied it in a small brochure with the somewhat fantastic title of 'A Study in Scarlet.'"
>
> He shook his head sadly. "I glanced over it," said he. "Honestly, I cannot congratulate you upon it. Detection is, or ought to be, an exact science, and should be treated in the same cold and unemotional manner. You have attempted to tinge it with romanticism, which produces much the same effect as if you worked a love-story or an elopement into the fifth proposition of Euclid."
>
> "But the romance was there," I remonstrated. "I could not tamper with the facts."
>
> "Some facts should be suppressed, or at least a just sense of proportion should be observed in treating them. The only point in the case which deserved mention was the curious analytical reasoning from effects to causes by which I succeeded in unravelling it."

How does Conan Doyle present Holmes's methods of detection in *The Sign of the Four*?

Write about:
• how Holmes's methods are presented in this extract, and
• how his methods are presented in the novel as a whole.

2) Read Chapter Two from "I sat in the window with the volume in my hand" to the end of the chapter, and then answer the question below.

Explore how Watson and Mary's romance is presented in *The Sign of the Four*. Refer to this extract, and to the novel as a whole.

3) Read Chapter Seven from the start of the chapter to "This Agra treasure intervened like an impassable barrier between us", and then answer the question below.

Explain how Watson is presented as an honourable character in this extract and in the novel as a whole.

Character Profile — Sherlock Holmes

Sherlock Holmes is the main character in the novel, so you don't need to be a detective to work out that you'll need to know him pretty darn well — there's a high chance you'll need to talk about him in the exam.

Holmes is a skilled detective

1) The story follows Holmes as he <u>skilfully</u> solves a <u>complex</u> case.

2) He describes himself as an "<u>unofficial consulting detective</u>" — he's not a member of the <u>police</u>, but he's sometimes called on to <u>help</u> them.

Holmes is...

Clever: "his analytical genius"

Rational: "that true cold reason which I place above all things"

Unfeeling: "You really are an automaton"

3) He is presented as <u>superior</u> to official detectives — he solves crimes that they <u>cannot</u>.

4) Holmes's skill is reflected in his <u>appearance</u> — his "<u>hawk-like features</u>" suggest that he <u>hunts</u> down criminals like a <u>bird of prey</u>.

© United Archives GmbH / Alamy Stock Photo

He has developed his own methods to solve mysteries

1) Holmes thinks that detective work "ought to be" an "<u>exact science</u>" — he has a <u>different</u> approach to solving cases than other detectives.

2) He is extremely <u>rational</u> and <u>logical</u>. He approaches cases like a <u>scientist</u> — he uses careful <u>observation</u> and <u>reasoning</u> to <u>deduce</u> the most likely solution.

Theme — Science

Sherlock's techniques are presented as the "<u>Science of Deduction</u>", which emphasises their precision and accuracy.

3) He has an "extraordinary genius for <u>minutiae</u>" — he pays attention to the tiny <u>details</u> that other people miss, such as the blood on the rope that Small used to get up to Bartholomew's window.

Holmes has <u>detailed</u> forensic knowledge — for example, he has written "several monographs", including one on different types of <u>tobacco ash</u>. This shows an almost <u>obsessive</u> approach to solving crime.

4) The <u>effectiveness</u> of Holmes's methods is established very early in the novel when he analyses Watson's watch — his deductions are so <u>accurate</u> that Watson accuses him of <u>finding out</u> the information about his brother beforehand and <u>pretending</u> to deduce it in some "fanciful way".

He is intelligent and talented

1) Holmes has a <u>detailed</u> knowledge of a <u>range</u> of <u>intellectual</u> subjects — he talks <u>knowledgeably</u> on "medieval pottery", "Stradivarius violins" and the "Buddhism of Ceylon".

2) Conan Doyle shows that Holmes is <u>well-read</u> and <u>well-educated</u> by having him discuss writers such as <u>Jean Paul Richter</u> (a German novelist) and <u>Winwood Reade</u> (a historian and philosopher).

3) He has <u>extensive</u> talents. He has a "<u>remarkable gift</u>" for the <u>violin</u> and can speak at least <u>two languages</u> — he discusses Jones in <u>French</u> and quotes the writer Goethe in <u>German</u>.

Writer's Techniques — Language

Doyle uses <u>sophisticated</u> language in Holmes's <u>dialogue</u> to reflect his <u>intelligence</u>. This makes him seem even more <u>impressive</u> to the reader.

4) Holmes's knowledge and skills are <u>greater</u> than those of the average reader, leaving the reader in <u>awe</u> of him.

Character Profile — Sherlock Holmes

He is happiest when he is solving cases

1) Holmes says that he "cannot live without brain-work" and asks "what else is there to live for?" This shows that he relies on detective work to feel fulfilled.

2) Detective work stimulates his brain in a way that ordinary life fails to do — he abhors the "dull routine of existence" and craves "mental exaltation."

3) Holmes is lively and enthusiastic when he is working on mysteries. After Mary Morstan comes to him with her case — he is "bright, eager, and in excellent spirits".

4) However, when he isn't working on a case, he has "fits of the blackest depression". He becomes lethargic and takes drugs in order to give his mind the stimulation it needs.

Theme — Duality

The contrasts in Holmes's mood and behaviour show the duality of his character — he is both a "loafer" and a "pretty spry sort of fellow".

Holmes's mood also suffers when he is stuck on a case. When there is no news of the Aurora, he paces his room and looks "worn and haggard". However, after he tracks it down, his "bright humour" results in a "merry" meal with Jones and Watson. This shows that getting results is vital to his wellbeing.

He is often cold and insensitive towards other people...

1) Holmes sees emotion as "antagonistic" to reasoning — it interferes with his ability to effectively solve cases. As a result, he chooses not to acknowledge his emotional side.

Conan Doyle presents Holmes as having an under-developed emotional side and a very well-developed rational side.

2) This means that Holmes is often cold and unfeeling:

Holmes can be caring — e.g. he shows concern that Watson is tired in Chapter Eight. This makes him a more rounded character.

• He criticises Watson's write-up of his last case, despite Watson's obvious desire to "please" Holmes.

• When Mary stops talking with a "choking sob", Holmes asks her more questions instead of comforting her.

• When Watson tells him he is getting married, he gives a "groan" and "cannot congratulate" him. Holmes says that he would never marry because love is an "emotional thing" which could "bias" his judgement.

... and he can be arrogant

1) Holmes has a very high opinion of himself and his deductive abilities. He calls himself "the only" detective of his kind "in the world" — he believes that he is unique.

2) He is dismissive of other detectives — he believes they are often "out of their depths". He tells Watson that he is "the last and highest court of appeal" — when other detectives can't solve a case, it is brought to him because he is the only one with the skills to solve it.

© Chris Wooley

3) Holmes often talks down to Watson. He patronisingly calls Watson "dear boy" and dismisses the case as "simplicity itself" when Watson can't understand it.

4) However, Holmes isn't interested in public credit for solving cases — the "work itself" is his "reward".

Write about the complexity of Holmes's character...

EXAM TIP

Make sure you can comment on all aspects of Holmes's character. Yes, he's a genius and all-round talented guy who loves to run round and solve mysteries, but he can also be moody, lazy and cold.

Character Profile — Dr John Watson

Watson is an ex-army doctor and Holmes's loyal assistant in solving the case. The two men are very different, but they're firm friends. It's a shame Watson puts a dent in this bromance when he falls in love with Mary.

Dr Watson is the novel's narrator

1) The story is told from Watson's <u>perspective</u> — the reader <u>only</u> has access to the <u>facts</u> and <u>insights</u> he reveals. Watson is not a brilliant detective like Holmes — Holmes has to <u>explain</u> his theories to him, which means they're explained to the <u>reader</u> too.

2) Watson can be seen as both a <u>reliable</u> and an <u>unreliable</u> narrator:

Watson is...

Eager: "Can I do anything? I am perfectly fresh now"

Loyal: "Sherlock Holmes was never at fault"

Caring: "I endeavoured to cheer and amuse her"

- He reports events in a <u>straightforward</u> way, and he is <u>honest</u> about his own <u>lack</u> of understanding — he says that the case is an "<u>insoluble mystery</u>" to him. This makes him seem <u>reliable</u>.
- However, his <u>admiration</u> of Holmes means that he is <u>biased</u> — his descriptions of Holmes are largely positive, e.g. he refers to his "<u>great powers</u>" and "<u>extraordinary qualities</u>".
- His <u>romanticism</u> also allows his <u>emotions</u> to <u>colour</u> his narrative — this is seen in his <u>glowing</u> description of <u>Mary</u> on their first meeting.

> Watson isn't blind to Holmes's flaws — he mentions Holmes's "vanity" and "egotism".

He is traditional...

> See pages 6-7 for more on typical Victorian beliefs.

Watson's character is portrayed as having <u>traditional</u> Victorian values:

1) He sees himself as "an army surgeon with a weak leg and a <u>weaker banking-account</u>". He believes that this means he will be <u>unable</u> to marry Mary because he wouldn't be able to <u>support</u> her <u>financially</u>.

2) Watson then worries that the treasure will put Mary "<u>forever beyond</u>" his reach. It would enable Mary to move in <u>higher social circles</u> and make her more likely to marry a <u>wealthy upper-class</u> man.

3) Watson <u>admires</u> Mary's "<u>perfect</u>" self-control and the way she remains calm in the "<u>angelic fashion of women</u>" after the events at Pondicherry Lodge.

4) When he updates Mary and Mrs Forrester on the case, he leaves out the "more <u>dreadful</u> parts of the <u>tragedy</u>" to <u>protect</u> them — he thinks they shouldn't be exposed to <u>unpleasant</u> things.

... and honourable

1) Watson does not want to <u>take advantage</u> of Mary's vulnerability — while she is "<u>weak</u> and <u>helpless</u>", he decides against telling her he loves her.

2) Mary's potential wealth <u>puts him off</u> asking her to marry him — he is not a "<u>fortune-seeker</u>".

3) He tries to do the <u>right thing</u> for Mary. Although he believes the treasure will put her out of his <u>reach</u>, he is ready to "<u>devote</u>" his life to finding it — he truly loves her and he wants her to have what is "<u>rightfully</u>" hers.

© ITV/REX/Shutterstock

> Watson's sense of honour means that he tries to <u>hide</u> his love from Mary. As a result, he comes across as "<u>cold</u> and <u>distant</u>". This shows that his sense of honour can have a <u>negative</u> impact on the way he <u>acts</u>.

Character Profile — Dr John Watson

He is loyal to Holmes and admires him

© Chris Wooley

1) Watson <u>admires</u> Holmes and has the "<u>greatest interest</u>" in his methods. Watson is <u>keen</u> to <u>observe</u> Holmes's work and <u>help</u> him.

2) Although the events at Pondicherry Lodge have "<u>shaken</u>" Watson, he wants to "<u>see the matter through</u>". He is <u>determined</u> to help Holmes even when he finds it <u>tough</u>.

3) Watson <u>unquestioningly</u> follows Holmes into <u>dangerous</u> situations — he takes part in the <u>boat chase</u> and <u>shoots</u> Tonga. Afterwards, it turns Watson "<u>sick</u>" to think of how <u>close</u> they came to <u>dying</u> from Tonga's dart — he doesn't think of the <u>danger</u> he is putting himself in at the time.

Theme — Science

Watson is an <u>intelligent</u> man himself — he is a <u>doctor</u>, and he <u>identifies</u> that Bartholomew Sholto was killed by a "powerful vegetable alkaloid."

He is the opposite of Holmes in many ways

1) Watson does not share Holmes's <u>flaws</u>:

- He <u>disapproves</u> of Holmes's drug-taking — he argues that Holmes shouldn't "<u>risk the loss</u>" of his "<u>great powers</u>" for a "<u>mere passing pleasure</u>".

- He is a <u>stable</u> character. He observes Holmes's changing <u>moods</u>, but is not <u>affected</u> by them and does not <u>experience</u> them himself. While Holmes becomes <u>restless</u> and "<u>feverish</u>" when the case stalls, Watson remains <u>calm</u> and tells Holmes that he is "<u>knocking</u>" <u>himself up</u> over it.

- Watson is <u>modest</u> when Mary tells him that she owes the treasure to him — he says that it was down to <u>Holmes</u>. This contrasts with the "<u>egotism</u>" that Watson observes in Holmes.

2) Watson is a <u>romantic</u> character — he is in touch with his <u>emotions</u>:

- Watson sees the romance in <u>everyday life</u>. When Holmes <u>criticises</u> Watson for the "<u>romanticism</u>" of the story he wrote about one of Holmes's cases, Watson argues that the "<u>romance was there</u>" — Watson was just writing the story as he <u>saw</u> it.

- His romantic character means that he is <u>open</u> to love — he <u>quickly</u> falls in love with Mary and proposes to her <u>shortly afterwards</u>.

- Watson <u>can't help</u> thinking about love. When Holmes gives him a <u>book to read</u>, his thoughts are "<u>far</u> from the daring speculations of the writer" — he <u>can't concentrate</u> on the book because he's thinking about <u>Mary</u>.

- He is able to <u>feel</u> emotions deeply and <u>express</u> them — he tells Mary that he loves her "<u>as truly as ever a man loved a woman</u>". When Holmes <u>fails</u> to even recognise that Mary is <u>attractive</u>, Watson calls him "<u>positively inhuman</u>" — he <u>can't understand</u> Holmes's lack of emotion.

Theme — Love

Watson <u>marvels</u> at love. His description of it as a "<u>wondrous subtle thing</u>" emphasises its <u>superiority</u> to <u>lowly</u> emotions explored in the novel, such as <u>greed</u> and <u>revenge</u>.

Write about the contrast between Watson and Holmes...

It's an important part of the novel. Be aware of their similarities too though. Watson might be sensible, but he enjoys a bit of risk like Holmes — Watson talks about enjoying the "wild thrill" of the boat chase.

Character Profile — Mary Morstan

Mary is the main female character in the novel. She provides Holmes with a case and Watson with love.

Mary is the catalyst for the story

1) Mary sets the plot <u>in motion</u> by coming to Holmes for help with <u>two mysteries</u> — the <u>disappearance</u> of her father and the anonymous gifts of <u>pearls</u> she has been receiving.

2) She <u>ably</u> tells Holmes the <u>facts</u> of the case and gives him <u>evidence</u> she has saved — this shows she is <u>intelligent</u>, and Holmes praises her for having "<u>correct intuition</u>".

3) For the rest of the novel, Mary's main role is as Watson's <u>love interest</u>. He is <u>immediately</u> attracted to her, but her feelings <u>aren't revealed</u> until the end of the novel. This adds <u>interest</u> and <u>suspense</u> to the subplot.

Mary is...

Intelligent: "She had a decided genius"

Composed: "her self-control was perfect"

Delicate: "She was weak and helpless, shaken in mind and nerve."

Writer's Techniques — Narrative

Watson's role as <u>narrator</u> means that the reader gets a <u>biased</u> view of Mary. But Holmes <u>praises</u> Mary too — he calls her "<u>charming</u>" and a "<u>model client</u>".

She is portrayed as the model Victorian woman

Mary <u>conforms</u> to how women were expected to <u>behave</u> and how they were <u>perceived</u> in Victorian times:

- **Composed:** Mary is <u>calm</u> and <u>controlled</u>. Even when Thaddeus insensitively reveals that her father is <u>dead</u>, she shows <u>little outward emotion</u> — she simply <u>sits</u> down and her face goes "<u>white</u> to the lips".
- **Dependent:** Mary instinctively turns to Watson for "<u>comfort</u> and <u>protection</u>" when she's scared, suggesting she <u>relies</u> on him.
- **Passive:** Mary does not take part in the <u>action</u> — she stays at <u>home</u> and <u>relies</u> on Watson to bring her news of the case.
- **Gentle and refined:** She has a "<u>sensitive</u>" nature. She dresses <u>tastefully</u>, and has a "<u>sweet</u>" and "<u>sympathetic</u>" expression.

Background and Context

In Victorian times, the <u>home</u> was seen as the <u>proper place</u> for women. Women were also viewed as needing <u>male protection</u> — Mary calls Holmes and Watson "<u>knight-errants</u>" who have come to her "<u>rescue</u>".

She values love over wealth

1) Mary appears to have "<u>limited means</u>" and the treasure would make her <u>rich</u>, but she shows "<u>no sign of elation</u>" at the prospect of this. She isn't <u>motivated</u> by money — this contrasts with the <u>greedy</u> characters who <u>do</u> want the treasure, including her own <u>father</u>.

2) Mary values Watson's <u>love</u> over the treasure — she echoes his "<u>Thank God</u>" when they find out the chest is empty because it means they can be <u>together</u>.

Theme — Love

A "<u>bright flush</u> of surprise and of <u>pleasure</u>" colours Mary's cheeks when Watson goes to see her — this <u>contrasts</u> with her reaction to the treasure, which she asks about "<u>coolly</u>".

© ITV/REX/Shutterstock

KEY QUOTE *"she turned so white that I feared that she was about to faint"*

Mary deals well with all the drama of the case — but ultimately she's portrayed as being weaker than the men, and Watson feels the need to offer her a cool beverage whenever she's about to keel over. Sigh.

Character Profile — Athelney Jones

Jones tries and fails to be a competent detective. So sad. It's pretty darn hilarious for the reader, though.

Jones is a strong contrast to Holmes

1) Jones is an official inspector of Scotland Yard, whereas Holmes is an "unofficial" private detective — this encourages the reader to compare the two men. Jones is a very different character to Holmes:

- Jones is presented as clumsy — his steps "sounded loudly" outside Bartholomew's room and he "strode heavily" inside. This contrasts with Holmes, who is "swift, silent and furtive".
- Jones's repetition and exclamations (e.g. "Bad business! Bad business!") contrast with Holmes's calm statements (e.g. "You are not quite in possession of the facts").
- Jones uses unscientific methods. He jumps to conclusions and tries to make the evidence fit his theory. Holmes makes reasoned deductions based on evidence.

> **Background and Context**
>
> The negative portrayal of the police reflects criticisms of police in the Victorian period (see p.6).

A foil is a character who contrasts with another character.

2) Jones is a foil to Holmes — the differences between them highlight Holmes's skill.

His attitude towards Holmes changes

© Chris Wooley

1) At first, Jones is dismissive of Holmes — he says that Holmes's success is more due to "luck than good guidance".

2) However, Jones also grudgingly admires Holmes — he can't hide that he is "impressed" by Holmes's description of the suspect.

3) Jones feels threatened by Holmes. Jones "snapped" at him and tells him not to "promise too much" when Holmes states that he can clear Thaddeus of murder. If Holmes is correct, it would prove that Jones is wrong and make him look incompetent.

4) Jones's attitude changes when he realises he needs Holmes's help. He becomes "meek and even apologetic", and calls Holmes a "wonderful man". However, he still acts in a superior way — he patronisingly says that Holmes would have made a "promising" officer.

5) After this, Jones is prepared to follow Holmes's orders, as long as Holmes leads him "to the men". Jones is happy to take the "official credit" — he is concerned with his reputation.

He is a comic character

1) Jones's mistakes and incompetence create humour — he makes incorrect arrests whilst criticising Holmes's far more effective methods.

2) Jones pompously portrays himself as a brilliant detective. When he theorises that Thaddeus is the murderer, he says "These flashes come upon me at times" — he acts as though he is blessed with inspiration.

3) Holmes pokes holes in Jones's theory — he suggests that Bartholomew "considerately got up" and locked the door after his death. This adds humour.

> **Jones is...**
>
> **Proud:** "my professional credit is at stake"
>
> **Pompous:** "My view of the case is confirmed."
>
> **Dismissive:** "It's Mr. Sherlock Holmes, the theorist."

EXAM TIP

Think about Jones's relationship with Holmes...

It's an interesting one. Jones admires Holmes and even works with him at the end, but he always acts in a superior way. He really wants to be seen as a good detective and feels threatened by Holmes.

Character Profile — Thaddeus Sholto

Pros: wants to right his father's wrongs. Cons: strange obsession with his heart. Well, we can't all be perfect.

Thaddeus is a fair man...

1) Thaddeus believes that Mary, as Captain Morstan's daughter, should get her <u>share</u> of the Agra treasure. He believes that she is a "<u>wronged</u>" woman who deserves "<u>justice</u>".

2) He <u>disapproves</u> of his brother Bartholomew's <u>greed</u>. Bartholomew doesn't want to share the treasure with Mary, but Thaddeus believes that they are her "<u>trustees</u>".

3) Thaddeus takes the "course which has seemed <u>right</u>" to him — he sends Mary <u>pearls</u>, tells her all he <u>knows</u> about the treasure and lets her know that it has finally been <u>found</u>.

> **Thaddeus is...**
>
> **Generous:** "We had plenty of money ourselves. I desired no more."
>
> **Nervous:** "Thaddeus Sholto... sat twitching on his luxurious settee."
>
> **Eccentric:** "Pray step into my little sanctum."

... but he is also self-obsessed

1) Thaddeus is a <u>hypochondriac</u> — he constantly <u>worries</u> about his own <u>health</u>. As soon as Watson introduces himself as a <u>doctor</u>, Thaddeus asks him to <u>listen</u> to his heart.

2) He is so <u>concerned</u> with his own health that he <u>doesn't consider</u> Mary's feelings when he "<u>airily</u>" mentions that her father died from "<u>throwing a strain</u>" upon his own heart.

3) Thaddeus lists "<u>interminable trains of symptoms</u>" on the drive to Pondicherry Lodge — he doesn't show any <u>interest</u> in anyone else.

4) His hypochondria has a <u>comic effect</u> — it makes him seem <u>ridiculous</u>.

© ITV/REX/Shutterstock

He adds to the mystery and unsettling mood

1) Thaddeus is at the <u>centre</u> of the Agra treasure <u>mystery</u> — this is reflected by his <u>home</u>:

- Thaddeus's house has a "<u>sorry</u>" outward appearance, but it is <u>richly</u> decorated inside with the "<u>glossiest</u>" curtains and "<u>richly-mounted</u>" paintings.
- His home is full of "<u>Eastern luxury</u>" such as "<u>Oriental</u>" vases and "great <u>tiger-skins</u>".

> **Background and Context**
>
> Thaddeus's eastern-themed home links him to the <u>British Empire</u>. Like the empire, his character is associated with both <u>exotic luxury</u> and <u>threat</u> (see p.43) — the treasure has led to the <u>deaths</u> of his father and brother.

2) The <u>precautions</u> he takes and the <u>anxiety</u> he shows <u>builds suspense</u>:

- He sends someone to make sure that Mary didn't bring "<u>unpleasant people</u>" (i.e. the police) with her.
- When he meets them, he seems <u>nervous</u> — he <u>twitches</u>, <u>shakes</u>, and his features "<u>jerk</u>" around.
- At Pondicherry Lodge, he is "<u>half blubbering with fear</u>".

KEY QUOTE

"I had quite high words with him last night"

Thaddeus isn't afraid to stand up for what he believes in — he even moved out of Pondicherry Lodge after arguing with Bartholomew about the treasure. This makes him seem principled and honourable.

Character Profile — Jonathan Small

Jonathan Small is a very vengeful man. I wouldn't even dare to use some of the milk out of his fridge.

Jonathan Small is the novel's antagonist

1) Small's desire for <u>revenge</u> on Major Sholto <u>drives</u> the story.

2) Despite his <u>importance</u>, the reader doesn't meet Small until the <u>final chapters</u> of the novel. The reader only gets <u>glimpses</u> of him from the reports of <u>other characters</u> — this makes him seem <u>mysterious</u>.

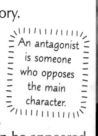

An antagonist is someone who opposes the main character.

© ITV/REX/Shutterstock

3) He is often portrayed in a <u>negative</u> way — for example, Thaddeus describes his eyes as "<u>wild</u>" and "<u>cruel</u>" when he <u>appeared</u> at Major Sholto's window. This makes him seem <u>threatening</u>.

He is manipulative, uncaring and violent...

1) Small <u>manipulates</u> Major Sholto. When he finds out that Sholto is losing a lot of money through <u>gambling</u>, he <u>uses</u> this fact to <u>tempt</u> Sholto with a <u>share</u> of the treasure in return for helping him escape.

2) He <u>takes advantage</u> of Tonga's <u>loyalty</u>. When he realises that Tonga is "<u>devoted</u>" to him, he uses him to <u>escape</u>. Small shows no real <u>concern</u> for Tonga — he doesn't <u>care</u> when Tonga dies.

Jonathan Small is...

Vengeful: "From that day I lived only for vengeance."

Frightening: "a terrible expression when moved to anger"

Loyal: "I have acted all through for them as much as for myself."

Theme — Crime

He commits this murder out of <u>vengeance</u> — he wants to <u>punish</u> the guard for "<u>insulting</u> and <u>injuring</u>" him.

3) Small <u>brutally</u> murders a convict-guard. The way he describes it shows his <u>cold</u> and <u>violent</u> nature — Small wanted to "<u>beat out his brains</u>", and he knocked "<u>the whole front of his skull in</u>".

4) He believes that the treasure is <u>rightfully</u> his — but he <u>stole</u> it just as <u>Sholto</u> stole it from him. This makes him seem <u>hypocritical</u>.

... but he isn't a straightforward villain

1) Small's <u>embedded narrative</u> in the last chapter gives details of his <u>background</u> — this <u>develops</u> his character and makes the reader feel <u>sympathy</u> for him. He has suffered <u>accidents</u> and <u>bad luck</u>:

- He is <u>disadvantaged</u> — his leg was <u>bitten off</u> by a crocodile, which left him a "<u>useless cripple</u>"
- He was caught up in the <u>Indian uprising</u>, which numbed him to <u>death</u> and <u>violence</u> — he became so used to "<u>meeting death at every turn</u>" that whether Achmet lived or died was "<u>a thing as light as air</u>" to him.

2) Small showed some <u>reluctance</u> about killing Achmet — he says that his "<u>heart softened</u>" towards him. This suggests that he has some <u>compassion</u> and isn't entirely <u>immoral</u>.

3) Small is extremely <u>loyal</u> to the three men he stole the treasure with — this shows a level of <u>integrity</u>.

4) He has a strong sense of <u>right</u> and <u>wrong</u> — his actions are motivated by Sholto's <u>betrayal</u>. The reader <u>judges</u> Sholto for his actions — it isn't just Small who has committed <u>evil</u> deeds.

KEY QUOTE

"a gleam of something like humour in his eyes"

The "humour" in Small's eyes makes him seem human — it is possible to feel some sympathy for him. He has reasons for doing the things he has done — you have to decide how much you judge him for them.

Character Profile — 'The Four' & Bartholomew

'The four' are Jonathan Small and his three co-conspirators — together, they steal the Agra treasure.
Some years later, the treasure falls into Bartholomew Sholto's hands. It doesn't do any of them any good...

'The four' are united by murder

1) Jonathan Small, Mahomet Singh, Abdullah Khan and Dost Akbar are all <u>linked</u> by the <u>murder</u> of Achmet and the <u>theft</u> of the treasure.

2) They are <u>violent</u> men. Small "<u>cast</u>" his gun between Achmet's legs and Dost Akbar "<u>buried his knife twice</u>" in Achmet's side.

3) However, they are <u>loyal</u> to each other — they <u>swear</u> an oath to always "<u>stand by each other</u>" after stealing the treasure. They <u>strengthen</u> this <u>oath</u> by calling themselves '<u>the four</u>' and drawing their sign — <u>four crosses</u>.

Writer's Techniques — Symbolism

The phrase and the crosses symbolise the <u>bond</u> between the men. The four crosses have their "arms touching" which represents the <u>closeness</u> of this bond.

4) They <u>remain</u> loyal to each other even when they are sent to <u>prison</u> for Achmet's murder. They all meet up to <u>discuss</u> terms with Sholto and swear more "<u>solemn oaths</u>".

'The Four' are...

United: "The four of us must always act together."

Brutal: "the other held a great knife to my throat"

Greedy: "There will be enough to make every one of us rich men"

© Chris Wooley

Bartholomew seems to be an unpleasant character

1) Bartholomew, Thaddeus's <u>twin</u> brother, is found dead in Chapter Five. The reader later learns that he was killed by <u>Tonga</u>, Small's <u>accomplice</u>, when Small and Tonga <u>stole</u> the treasure back from Bartholomew.

Bartholomew is...

Rich: "We had plenty of money ourselves."

Greedy: "a little inclined to my father's fault"

Intelligent: "Bartholomew is a clever fellow"

2) The reader never meets Bartholomew <u>alive</u>. All the information they learn about him is <u>third-hand</u> — it comes from <u>Watson's</u> account of <u>Thaddeus's</u> narrative. The reader's opinion of Bartholomew is affected by Watson's views — he hears "<u>little good</u>" of Bartholomew, so feels "<u>no intense antipathy</u>" to his murderers.

3) Thaddeus claims that Bartholomew is <u>greedy</u>, like their <u>father</u>. Bartholomew <u>doesn't agree</u> with Thaddeus that they should <u>share</u> the treasure with Mary — he is "<u>averse</u>" to sending her the pearls.

Theme — Duality

Thaddeus and Bartholomew can be seen as <u>opposites</u>. Thaddeus is the <u>good</u> brother — he is <u>generous</u> and tries to do <u>right</u>. Bartholomew is the <u>bad</u> brother — he is <u>greedy</u> and <u>selfish</u>.

4) Thaddeus describes how Bartholomew became "<u>very angry</u>" with him for wanting to share the treasure with Mary — he says that Bartholomew is a "<u>terrible fellow</u>" when angry. This makes Bartholomew seem <u>unreasonable</u> and <u>frightening</u>.

Bartholomew is <u>similar</u> to his father, <u>Major Sholto</u> — Thaddeus describes Bartholomew as the "<u>favourite son</u>" and believes that their father told Bartholomew "<u>more</u> than he ever told" Thaddeus. This <u>associates</u> Bartholomew with the <u>greed</u> and <u>wrongdoing</u> of his father.

KEY QUOTE

"We have sworn it. The four of us must always act together."

Sure, 'the four' are pretty unpleasant in many ways — violent, money-grabbing and much too free with their knives. But they're totally loyal to one another and look out for each other through thick and thin.

Character Profile — Major Sholto & Captain Morstan

Major Sholto and Captain Morstan make a deal with Small to free him and his three co-conspirators from prison for a share of the Agra treasure. However, their greed over the treasure brings them to a sticky end...

Major Sholto is motivated by greed

Major Sholto is...

Greedy: "The cursed greed which has been my besetting sin"

Untrustworthy: "The scoundrel had stolen it all"

Haunted by fear: "He was very fearful of going out alone"

1) Sholto has a "struggle" with his moral principles when Small first tells him about the treasure, but his greed overpowers him — he decides to bargain with Small instead of telling him to report it to the government.

2) Small offers Sholto and Morstan a "fifth share" of the treasure, but Sholto calls this "not very tempting" — he wants more. He then steals the treasure for himself, despite inheriting a "fortune" from his uncle.

Theme — Greed

Sholto can't even overcome his greed on his deathbed. He admits that half of the treasure "should have been" Mary's, but he tells his sons to send her "nothing" until after he dies in case he recovers.

3) Sholto "clung" on to Morstan's share after he died. He couldn't bear to share it because the "mere feeling of possession" was important to him — he didn't use the treasure, he just wanted to own it.

4) Sholto's greed results in his death — Small tracks him down and Sholto dies from the shock of seeing him.

He is a disloyal friend

1) Sholto betrays Morstan, who is supposed to be his "bosom" friend — this shows that Sholto values the treasure over their friendship.

2) Sholto covers up Morstan's death. He is selfishly more worried about being "accused" of murder and people finding out about the treasure than about acting honourably towards his friend by confessing.

© Chris Wooley

Captain Morstan takes advantage of the treasure

1) Morstan is also shown to be greedy and corrupt — although not to the same extent as Sholto.

2) He is aware the treasure is a "dirty business". However, he joins Sholto in making the deal with Small anyway — he thinks that the treasure will help them with their gambling losses.

Captain Morstan is...

Opportunistic: "the money would save our commissions handsomely"

Weary: "He came home with his heart full of hope, to find some peace, some comfort"

Both Morstan and Sholto die before the novel begins. The reader only learns about them from other characters, but Morstan is talked about less than Sholto, so his character is more of a mystery.

3) Morstan's greed leads to his death too — he dies while arguing with Sholto over how to divide the treasure.

4) The reader feels some sympathy for Morstan. He is wronged by Sholto, and he is shown to have a caring side — his message to Mary is "full of kindness and love".

EXAM TIP

Write about symbolism...

In the exam, you could comment on the not-massively-subtle symbolism of Captain Morstan's death. He dies after hitting his head on the treasure chest — this represents the dangers of being greedy.

Character Profile — Other Characters

Just two more pages of characters to get stuck into. These ones might not get a whole page each, but they're still important. Make sure you know who they are and why Conan Doyle included them in the novel.

Tonga is badly treated in the novel

1) Tonga is a <u>native</u> of the <u>Andaman Islands</u>. He helps Small <u>escape</u> and becomes his <u>accomplice</u>.

2) He is presented as <u>vicious</u>, and he commits some <u>evil</u> acts — he <u>kills</u> Bartholomew and <u>tries to kill</u> Holmes and Watson.

3) The characters in the novel are very <u>prejudiced</u> against Tonga. They think he is <u>savage</u> and <u>inhuman</u> — Small calls him a "<u>blood-thirsty imp</u>" and Watson describes him as having a "<u>half animal fury</u>". This depiction of Tonga reflects the <u>Victorian belief</u> that inhabitants of the colonies were <u>uncivilised</u> and <u>dangerous</u>.

> **Writer's Techniques — Imagery**
>
> <u>Animal imagery</u> is often used to <u>describe</u> Tonga — e.g. Small says that he was "<u>as venomous as a young snake</u>". This emphasises that the characters in the novel don't see Tonga as <u>human</u>.

4) Tonga is extremely <u>loyal</u> to Small, but he is <u>mistreated</u> by him:

- He is exhibited at <u>fairs</u> by Small as the "<u>black cannibal</u>" to make money — this is <u>demeaning</u>.
- Small "<u>welted</u>" Tonga with the end of a rope for <u>killing</u> Bartholomew.

5) <u>Nobody</u> shows any <u>sorrow</u> or <u>regret</u> at Tonga's death — not even Small, who was supposed to be his <u>friend</u>. Watson <u>unfeelingly</u> thinks about Tonga lying somewhere "<u>in the dark ooze</u>" of the Thames. This shows how <u>little</u> the characters in the novel <u>value</u> Tonga's life.

> **Theme — Imperialism**
>
> Watson refers to Tonga as "<u>that strange visitor</u>" — Tonga's death symbolises how the British characters have <u>successfully</u> removed a <u>dangerous</u> foreign influence from Britain and reasserted their <u>dominance</u>.

Mrs Cecil Forrester and Mrs Hudson are caring women

1) Mrs Cecil Forrester <u>employs</u> Mary Morstan as a governess.

- She treats Mary as an "<u>honoured friend</u>" rather than an <u>employee</u> — she <u>sits up</u> and <u>waits</u> until 2am for Mary to <u>return</u> from her meeting with Holmes, and she acts "<u>tenderly</u>" towards Mary.
- She is portrayed as a source of <u>comfort</u> during the case — Watson says that it is "<u>soothing</u>" to see her "<u>tranquil English home</u>" during the "<u>wild, dark business</u>" of the mystery.

> **Writer's Techniques — Symbolism**
>
> Mrs Forrester's home is presented as a beacon of "<u>shining</u>" light — it symbolises <u>peace</u> and <u>domesticity</u> in contrast to the "<u>dark</u>" nature of the case. Her <u>English</u> home also contrasts with the <u>exotic settings</u> of the novel.

© ITV/REX/Shutterstock

2) Mrs Hudson is Holmes and Watson's <u>landlady</u>.

- She shows <u>concern</u> for Holmes — she <u>anxiously</u> pays attention to his walking "up and down" and "muttering" to himself, and tells Watson that she is "<u>afraid for his health</u>".
- She puts up with <u>a lot</u> from Holmes. She wails with "<u>dismay</u>" at the noisy arrival of the Baker Street irregulars, and says that Holmes "<u>turned on her</u>" with "<u>such a look</u>" when he was in a bad mood — this shows she is <u>tolerant</u>.

> **Background and Context**
>
> These characters reflect how Victorian women were <u>passive</u> and associated with <u>domesticity</u>. They remain in their <u>homes</u> and are not involved in the <u>action</u>.

Character Profile — Other Characters

Mr Sherman and Toby are very useful to Holmes...

Mr Sherman is one of Holmes's acquaintances. Holmes sends Watson to Sherman's house to collect a sniffer dog, Toby, who Holmes believes will be able to track the creosote on Tonga's foot.

SHERMAN

- Sherman is working class and eccentric. He lives in a "shabby" brick house where he keeps lots of animals, such as badgers, stoats and birds.
- Sherman's character shows the wide variety of contacts that Holmes has and his influence over them. Sherman is hostile to Watson at first, but when Watson mentions Holmes's name it has a "magical effect" on Sherman and he immediately invites Watson inside.

TOBY

- Toby has the "most amazing power of scent". He is eventually able to follow Tonga's trail despite the time that has elapsed and the "great traffic" that has passed.
- His appearance and actions provide comic relief — he has a "clumsy waddling gait" and initially leads Holmes and Watson to a creosote barrel in a timber yard rather than to Small and Tonga.
- Toby highlights the unusual but effective methods that Holmes has at his disposal.

... as are the Baker Street irregulars

1) The Baker Street irregulars are a group of street urchins led by an older boy, Wiggins. They are another example of the unusual methods that Holmes uses — he pays them to look for the Aurora.

2) They are scruffy and unruly — Watson describes them as "dirty and ragged" boys who make a "tumultuous entry" to Baker Street. However, they seem to respect Holmes — they make "some show of discipline" once they are inside his home.

© ITV/REX/Shutterstock

3) Holmes regards them as more effective than the police — he says that he would call on the police "at the last moment" for help, whereas he praises how the Baker Street irregulars can "go everywhere, see everything, overhear every one".

The Smiths are a working-class family

1) Mordecai Smith owns a wharf and lives next to it in a "small brick house" with his wife and sons. He hires the Aurora out to Small, and Holmes questions his wife to try and find out where the boat is.

2) Mrs Smith is easily manipulated by Holmes — she tells Holmes everything she knows about Small and the Aurora, even though Holmes is a total stranger to her.

3) Mordecai Smith likes a drink — he spends the money that Small pays him for the Aurora in alehouses and is "rather the worse for liquor" when Holmes sees him at Jacobson's Yard.

4) The Smiths aren't intelligent. Watson sarcastically refers to their young son as "the prodigy" after he slowly answers Holmes's questions.

Background and Context

The Smiths reflect Victorian attitudes to working-class people. Holmes refers to them dismissively as "people of that sort".

EXAM TIP

Mention some of the minor characters in your exam...

Including some relevant points about minor characters will help you to show a firm understanding of the novel. Make sure you're confident writing about Tonga — he is especially important to the novel's themes.

Practice Questions

Sherlock Holmes may take centre stage with his fancy forensic techniques and his impossible deductions, but there's more to the novel than just his character. For top marks, you need to get to grips with all the characters in the novel — they're all important. Give these questions a go to see how well you really know them all.

Quick Questions

1) Write down three features of Holmes's personality.

2) Find a quote that suggests Watson is honourable.

3) Give two ways in which Mary is important to the plot.

4) Give three examples that show the contrast between Jones and Holmes.

5) a) Give one aspect of Thaddeus's character that is comical.
   b) Give one way in which Thaddeus's character adds to the unsettling mood of the novel.

6) Describe Small's character in one sentence.

7) Briefly explain how 'the four' show loyalty to each other.

8) Find two quotes from the novel which show that Bartholomew is an unpleasant character.

9) a) Give one similarity in the way Major Sholto and Captain Morstan are presented.
   b) Give one difference in the way Major Sholto and Captain Morstan are presented.

10) Give two examples which show that other characters are prejudiced against Tonga.

11) How does Conan Doyle use the character of Toby to create humour?

In-depth Questions

1) Describe Holmes's character, using quotes to back up your answer.

2) Do you think Watson is a reliable narrator? Give reasons for your answer.

3) How does Conan Doyle portray Mary's attitude towards the Agra treasure?
   Use evidence from the text to explain your answer.

4) How does the character of Jones change throughout the novel?
   Use quotations from the text to back up your answer.

5) How does Conan Doyle present Small as a vengeful man?
   Use evidence from the text to support your answer.

Practice Questions

What a treat — more questions to get your teeth into. These are great preparation for the questions you'll have to face in the exam — the more you do now, the more confident you'll feel when it comes to the big day, which will be nice. Don't forget to back up all your points with quotes and explain them clearly.

Exam-style Questions

1) Read the following extract from Chapter Nine ('A Break in the Chain'), and then answer the question that follows.

> "I don't think that you have any cause to be uneasy, Mrs. Hudson," I answered. "I have seen him like this before. He has some small matter upon his mind which makes him restless." I tried to speak lightly to our worthy landlady, but I was myself somewhat uneasy when through the long night I still from time to time heard the dull sound of his tread, and knew how his keen spirit was chafing against this involuntary inaction.
>
> At breakfast-time he looked worn and haggard, with a little fleck of feverish colour upon either cheek.
>
> "You are knocking yourself up, old man," I remarked. "I heard you marching about in the night."
>
> "No, I could not sleep," he answered. "This infernal problem is consuming me. It is too much to be balked by so petty an obstacle, when all else had been overcome. I know the men, the launch, everything; and yet I can get no news. I have set other agencies at work, and used every means at my disposal. The whole river has been searched on either side, but there is no news, nor has Mrs. Smith heard of her husband. I shall come to the conclusion soon that they have scuttled the craft. But there are objections to that."
>
> "Or that Mrs. Smith has put us on a wrong scent."
>
> "No, I think that may be dismissed. I had inquiries made, and there is a launch of that description."
>
> "Could it have gone up the river?"
>
> "I have considered that possibility too, and there is a search-party who will work up as far as Richmond. If no news comes to-day, I shall start off myself to-morrow, and go for the men rather than the boat. But surely, surely, we shall hear something."

How does Conan Doyle present the similarities and differences between Holmes and Watson in *The Sign of the Four*? Refer to the extract and to the rest of the novel.

2) Read Chapter Seven from "It was nearly two o'clock" to "... which had absorbed us". Explore how Conan Doyle presents the ideal of Victorian womanhood in this extract and in the rest of the novel.

3) Explore how Conan Doyle presents Jonathan Small as both a criminal and a victim in *The Sign of the Four*.

4) Read Chapter Ten from "At the sound of his strident, angry cries" to "I caught one glimpse of his venomous, menacing eyes amid the white swirl of the waters". How does Conan Doyle present Tonga in this extract and in the rest of the novel?

Crime and Justice

Crime forms the backdrop of the story — it's often motivated by lovely human qualities like greed and revenge. However, some criminals are victims of crime too, and they're desperate to get some justice.

Some crime is motivated by greed

See p.44 for more on the theme of greed.

1) Small agreed to help steal the Agra treasure partly out of greed. He told Abdullah Khan that he was "as ready to be rich as you can be".

Character — Jonathan Small

Small's actions were influenced by his circumstances. He saw himself as a "useless cripple" after he lost his leg and thought about what his family would think when they saw "their ne'er-do-well" coming back from India rich — he wanted to impress his family and secure a good future for himself.

2) It was this greed that helped him overcome his doubts about killing Achmet. Thinking about committing murder gave Small "chills", but when he "thought of the treasure" his "heart set as hard as flint".

3) Greed also motivated Major Sholto's crimes:

- He betrayed Morstan and Small, and stole the treasure for himself, even though his uncle had left him a "fortune" — he didn't need the money, he just wanted it out of greed.

- Greed stopped him reporting Morstan's death. He was worried that if he did, people would find out about the treasure, which he was "particularly anxious to keep secret" — he wanted to keep all of it for himself.

Small is willing to commit crime for vengeance

1) Small wanted to kill Major Sholto to get revenge on him.

2) He couldn't bear to feel that Sholto was "at his ease in a palace" with money that Small believed was rightfully his — he thought that he had been wronged by Sholto.

3) When pursuing Sholto, Small cared "nothing for the gallows" — his need for vengeance consumed him so much that he didn't care about the legality or consequences of his actions.

4) Small's desire for revenge is more powerful than his greed — he says that the Agra treasure had come to be "a smaller thing" in his mind than "slaying" Sholto.

© Chris Wooley

Unlike Sholto, whose greed meant that he could never part with the treasure, Small is willing to never see it again as long as he gets revenge — he throws it in the Thames to stop it going to "kith or kin of Sholto or of Morstan".

Tonga's motives for crime are less clear

1) It seems that Tonga killed Bartholomew partly out of loyalty to Small. He thought that killing Bartholomew was what Small wanted, and he "would do anything to serve" him.

After committing the murder, Tonga struts around "as proud as a peacock" — he thinks Small will be pleased with him.

2) However, it seems that Tonga is primarily driven to crime by his "blood-thirsty" nature — Holmes says that Bartholomew was killed because Tonga's "savage instincts" broke out.

Background and Context

This portrayal of Tonga reflects the prejudiced Victorian belief that people from the colonies were barbaric. Tonga is presented as inherently violent, which leads him to commit crime. In contrast, British characters are shown to have clear motives for crime, such as greed and revenge.

Crime and Justice

Legal justice is portrayed as ineffective

1) In the novel, the police do not seem <u>capable</u> of securing justice. While Holmes is portrayed as a "<u>connoisseur of crime</u>" (a crime expert), Inspector Athelney Jones is a pompous, bumbling and comic character, whose "normal state" is to be <u>out of his depth</u>.

Background and Context

Conan Doyle's portrayal of an <u>ineffective</u> police force mirrors <u>public opinion</u> about the London police in the late 19th century. The force was criticised for its mistakes in the 1888 <u>Jack the Ripper</u> case (see p.6).

2) Jones unwittingly works <u>against</u> justice by <u>arresting</u> Thaddeus. In <u>contrast</u>, Holmes aims to correct this injustice by finding the <u>actual</u> culprits so that he can "<u>clear</u>" Thaddeus's name.

3) Jones only <u>accidentally</u> catches criminals. He hastily arrests everyone at Pondicherry Lodge, including the butler, <u>Lal Rao</u> — it later turns out the butler was working for <u>Small</u>.

Personal justice is presented as both bad and good

1) Small's idea of personal justice is <u>flawed</u> — he believes that, unlike Major Sholto, he "<u>earned</u>" the treasure through his <u>suffering</u> in the Andamans. However, he was <u>imprisoned</u> there for helping to <u>kill</u> a man who was <u>rightfully</u> guarding the treasure.

2) Small's attempts to get justice required <u>more crime</u> — he would have <u>murdered</u> the Major, and he <u>stole</u> the treasure again.

3) Holmes's type of personal justice is <u>admired</u> — he is an "<u>unofficial detective</u>" who secures justice for others by <u>skilfully</u> solving crimes. His pursuit of justice <u>blocks</u> Small's attempts to get personal justice — he <u>catches</u> Small and <u>stops</u> him from escaping with the treasure.

© Chris Wooley

Most characters get what they deserve

1) **Major Sholto** was <u>punished</u> for stealing the treasure — but not by the <u>law</u>. His crime <u>negatively</u> affected his life and led to his early <u>death</u>. He lived in <u>fear</u> that Small would track him down and <u>died</u> from the shock of seeing him.

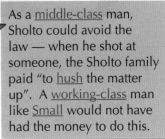

As a <u>middle-class</u> man, Sholto could avoid the law — when he shot at someone, the Sholto family paid "to <u>hush</u> the matter up". A <u>working-class</u> man like <u>Small</u> would not have had the money to do this.

2) **Jonathan Small** doesn't get the justice he thinks he <u>deserves</u> — he doesn't get to <u>keep</u> the treasure, and he is put in <u>prison</u>. However, no-one else can have the treasure — to him, that is a kind of justice. Holmes hopes to "<u>prove</u>" that Small didn't kill Bartholomew — he doesn't want him to be <u>punished</u> for a crime that he <u>didn't commit</u>.

3) **Mary Morstan** doesn't get the justice that <u>Thaddeus</u> wants for her — she doesn't get a <u>share</u> of the treasure. However, this is portrayed as a <u>good</u> thing — the treasure has brought people nothing but <u>harm</u>. It is the loss of the treasure that allows Mary to be with <u>Watson</u>, and this can also be seen as a kind of justice.

EXAM TIP

Don't forget to write about context...

You could weave a comment into your answer about how crime was associated with the working classes in the Victorian era. Small reflects this — he's a working-class man who ends up in prison twice.

Science

In case you hadn't noticed, Holmes likes science — a lot. He goes around shouting sciencesciencescience all the time. But seriously, Holmes's scientific approach is what makes him such a good detective.

Holmes uses scientific knowledge to gather evidence...

1) Holmes believes that having a "wide range of <u>exact knowledge</u>" is essential to being a <u>good</u> detective.

2) He has <u>extensive</u> knowledge of <u>forensic science</u> — he can tell apart different types of <u>tobacco ash</u>, analyse people's <u>footprints</u> and work out someone's profession from their <u>hands</u>. He has even <u>written texts</u> on these subjects.

3) Holmes uses <u>forensic methods</u> at crime scenes. On the windowsill at Pondicherry Lodge, he identifies the "impression of a <u>wooden stump</u>" and <u>uses</u> this evidence to make deductions. In contrast, Jones doesn't collect evidence — he just <u>guesses</u> and comes to the <u>wrong</u> conclusion.

Background and Context

Forensic investigation was in its <u>infancy</u> in the late 19th century — <u>fingerprinting</u> wasn't officially adopted by Scotland Yard until <u>1901</u>. Before this, convictions often relied on <u>eyewitness testimony</u>. Victorian readers would have admired Holmes's <u>innovative</u> scientific methods.

... and uses logic and reason to arrive at conclusions

© Collection Christophel/ ArenaPAL

1) Holmes comes to his conclusions in a <u>scientific</u> way. He weighs up the <u>evidence</u> and methodically <u>eliminates</u> unlikely explanations until he is left with the <u>most likely</u> one. This is shown to be a <u>reliable</u> method.

2) In Chapter One, Holmes <u>deduces</u> that Watson has been to the post office. <u>Impressively</u>, he even deduces the <u>specific</u> post office from the mould on Watson's shoes. He concludes that Watson went there to send a telegram after <u>observing</u> that he had not written a letter and didn't need to buy any stamps or postcards.

3) Holmes is <u>critical</u> of those who use "<u>guess-work</u>" instead of <u>logic</u> — he calls it a "<u>shocking habit</u>". This makes scientific methods seem <u>superior</u>.

Logic is the science of reasoning.

This scientific approach makes Holmes a better detective

1) Holmes's belief that detection should be an "<u>exact science</u>" sets him <u>apart</u> from other detectives like Jones — while they are "<u>out of their depths</u>", he is able to examine the "<u>data</u>" and give a "<u>specialist's</u>" opinion".

2) Jones doesn't even seem to <u>understand</u> Holmes's scientific methods. Jones <u>mockingly</u> calls Holmes "<u>the theorist</u>" because he doesn't appreciate his use of logic and reason — he thinks that Holmes just comes up with <u>wild theories</u>.

3) Ironically, it's <u>Jones</u> who comes up with foolish theories. He says that "<u>Facts are better</u>" than Holmes's "<u>theories</u>", but he <u>ignores</u> the facts and <u>incorrectly</u> reasons that Thaddeus killed Bartholomew.

Character — Sherlock Holmes

Science is shown to be <u>integral</u> to Holmes's character. When he is <u>frustrated</u>, he gives his mind a "<u>thorough rest</u>" by performing a chemical experiment. This shows that he finds <u>comfort</u> and <u>relief</u> in science.

Write about Conan Doyle's use of language...

Conan Doyle includes scientific terms, such as "hydrocarbon" and "rigor mortis", in Holmes's speech. Mention how this highlights Holmes's scientific knowledge and gives the reader confidence in his abilities.

Rationality vs Emotion

Conan Doyle explores the tension between rationality and emotion in *The Sign of the Four*. The characters in the novel show rationality and emotion to different extents — they're all such complicated little souls.

Holmes displays an interesting mix of rationality and emotion

1) Holmes values reason "above all things" and thinks that emotion is "opposed" to reason — emotion has a negative impact on his ability to be logical. He doesn't believe he can be both rational and emotional.

2) As a result, he responds to things in a very unemotional way. Whereas Watson notices that Mary is "attractive", Holmes only sees her as a client. To him, she is "a mere unit, — a factor in a problem".

3) However, it seems that Holmes does have an emotional side that exists alongside his rationality. He has formed a successful relationship with Watson and clearly cares about him — in Chapter Eight, Holmes worries that Watson is tired and puts him to sleep by playing the violin.

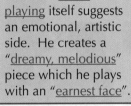

Holmes's violin playing itself suggests an emotional, artistic side. He creates a "dreamy, melodious" piece which he plays with an "earnest face".

4) Holmes also has a less stable emotional side. He becomes depressed and irritable when he doesn't have cases to solve (see p.25) — it is as though his rational thinking during cases keeps these negative emotions under control.

Watson's rationality and emotion contrasts with Holmes's

1) Watson usually responds to things in a more emotional way than Holmes. He is affected by the "dull, heavy" atmosphere on the journey to the theatre, whereas Holmes can "rise superior" to such things.

2) Watson can easily form strong emotional attachments. This is shown through Mary — he likes her as soon as he meets her, and he quickly grows to love her "as truly as ever a man loved a woman".

3) Watson's emotional intelligence seems to come at the expense of his reasoning skills — he's not a talented detective like Holmes.

Theme — Duality

Watson's rational side contrasts with Holmes's less stable emotional side. See p.42 for more on their duality.

4) However, Watson does have a rational side — this is apparent when he reasons with Holmes about the risks of drug-taking.

Women are presented as highly emotional

1) Watson thinks Mary must be "more than a woman" because she shows perfect "self-control". This reflects the Victorian view that women were less able to control their emotions than men.

© ITV/REX/Shutterstock

2) The female characters often have emotional outbursts, which makes them seem overly sensitive and irrational. For example:

- Mrs Bernstone is "hysterical" after she sees Bartholomew's body. Her speech contains lots of exclamations, such as "Oh, but I have been sorely tried this day!", which emphasises her agitation.
- Mary breaks down into "a passion of weeping" on the way home from Pondicherry Lodge, even though she hasn't seen the crime scene. This reaction suggests that her emotions are stronger than her self-control.

KEY QUOTE

"emotional qualities are antagonistic to clear reasoning"

Holmes believes that if he allowed himself to feel emotions in the same way that Watson does, his ability to think logically would be affected. And if he couldn't solve the case, it would be a pretty unsatisfying novel...

Duality

Duality is when someone or something has two parts that are in opposition to each other. The novel explores this through contrasting pairs of characters, and characters who contain contrasts within themselves.

Conan Doyle uses Holmes and Watson to explore duality

1) Holmes and Watson are very <u>different</u> — Holmes is <u>mainly rational</u>, whereas Watson is <u>mainly emotional</u>.

© John Timbers / ArenaPAL

2) There are contrasts <u>within</u> Holmes's character, too:

- When Holmes is working on cases, his mind is <u>focused</u> and <u>rational</u>, but when his mind <u>stagnates</u>, he becomes <u>emotional</u> and <u>erratic</u>.
- Holmes recognises this and quotes Goethe (a German writer) to describe himself, which translates as "Nature, alas, made only <u>one</u> of you although there was material for a <u>good man</u> and a <u>rogue</u>". This means that Holmes has both <u>good</u> and <u>bad</u> inside him.
- Holmes's <u>duality</u> emphasises his <u>complexity</u> and makes him seem <u>unpredictable</u>. For example, his past as a <u>fighter</u> is <u>surprising</u> — it's hard to imagine the <u>intellectual</u> Holmes taking part in a <u>violent</u> sport.

Holmes and Athelney Jones are very different detectives

1) Holmes and Jones both pursue <u>criminals</u>. However, their <u>characters</u> and <u>approaches</u> are presented as <u>opposites</u>. This emphasises Holmes's <u>skill</u> as a detective.

- Holmes <u>reasons</u> carefully, whereas Jones <u>jumps</u> to the <u>wrong</u> conclusions — Jones has <u>barely arrived</u> at Bartholomew's house to investigate his death when he exclaims "<u>Ha! I have a theory</u>".
- While Holmes is <u>calm</u> and <u>collected</u>, Jones <u>rushes</u> around the room. This makes Jones look <u>foolish</u>.

2) Holmes and Jones are in <u>opposition</u> — each has <u>confidence</u> in their own ability and <u>looks down</u> on the other. This opposition <u>breaks down</u> later in the novel when Jones seems "<u>apologetic</u>" after Thaddeus is proven innocent. This emphasises Holmes's <u>superiority</u>.

> **Writer's Techniques — Language**
>
> Conan Doyle uses lots of <u>exclamation marks</u> in Jones's speech at Pondicherry Lodge. This creates a <u>loud</u>, <u>brash</u> first impression, which contrasts with Holmes's <u>quiet</u> confidence.

The Sholto twins are opposites

1) Thaddeus is <u>moral</u> — he believes that he and his brother are Miss Morstan's "trustees" and that they have a <u>responsibility</u> to <u>share</u> their father's treasure with her.

2) However, Bartholomew has his "<u>father's fault</u>" (<u>greed</u>) and doesn't want to share the treasure with Mary. This makes him seem <u>dishonourable</u>.

3) The fact that the brothers are <u>identical twins</u> is significant. They look exactly the <u>same</u>, which makes them seem like <u>the same person</u>. This emphasises that people have both <u>good</u> and <u>bad</u> in them — <u>Thaddeus</u> represents the <u>good half</u> and <u>Bartholomew</u> the <u>bad half</u>.

> **Writer's Techniques — Form**
>
> The idea of the '<u>double</u>' is a <u>common theme</u> in <u>gothic fiction</u>, e.g. *Jekyll and Hyde* and *Frankenstein*. It was used to explore the idea that people are made up of both <u>good</u> and <u>bad</u>.

Comment on Conan Doyle's use of duality...

There's a lot of duality in the novel that you could comment on in the exam. Englishness vs. foreignness is another good one — but remember that Victorians had different views of foreignness to modern readers.

Imperialism

Imperialism is the policy of countries gaining power over other countries (see p.8). Britain used to be pretty serious about imperialism — by the 19th century, its empire (which included India) was big and powerful.

The novel portrays the empire as wealthy and exotic...

1) The Agra treasure represents India's wealth. Abdullah Khan persuaded Jonathan Small to help steal it by telling him it would make him rich, an aim he described as "that which your countrymen come to this land for." This reflects how the Victorians saw the empire as a source of wealth. Khan's words may also be an ironic comment on the Victorian belief that British people were entitled to the riches of their colonies.

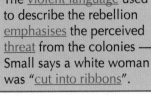
© ITV/REX/Shutterstock

2) Thaddeus's Indian-themed home contains foreign items such as "great tiger-skins" and a "hookah". This makes India seem exotic. Thaddeus's interest in India reflects the fascination that some Victorians had with other cultures in the empire.

> A hookah is a type of smoking pipe that was often associated with India.

... but it is also portrayed as a threat

Writer's Techniques

The violent language used to describe the rebellion emphasises the perceived threat from the colonies — Small says a white woman was "cut into ribbons".

1) Jonathan Small talks about the "great mutiny" that made India into a "perfect hell". He is referring to the 1857 rebellion against British colonial rule in India (see p.8). This was a bloody conflict started by Indian soldiers. It was a threat to Britain's imperial power and to British people living in India.

Background and Context

The novel reflects the differing attitudes towards empire — it was a source of both fascination and fear for Victorians.

2) Victorians also worried that foreign culture would corrupt what they believed were 'superior' British values — being British implied certain standards, like honour and decency. It was foreign treasure that tempted Sholto to sacrifice his honour by betraying his promise to Small.

3) Tonga coming to Britain symbolises the fear some Victorians had that Britain was unable to protect itself against foreigners and foreign influences. This makes him a threatening figure in the novel.

The novel reflects imperialistic attitudes

1) **Britain exploited India for its wealth and resources:**
   Small exhibits Tonga as a fairground attraction in order to make money. Sholto feels entitled to take the treasure from 'the four' and India — he just sees it as a chance to get rich.

2) **Many Victorians believed that people from the colonies were 'savages':**
   Small describes the inhabitants of the Andaman Islands as "wild cannibal natives". Watson describes Tonga's face as marked with "bestiality" and "cruelty".

3) **Victorians believed in Britain's 'civilising' influence over people from the colonies:**
   Holmes reads from a book that says British officials tried and "failed" to "win" over Andaman 'natives' — they wanted to make them less hostile.

People from the Andaman Islands are portrayed as 'immune' to British influence. This reinforces Tonga's depiction as a 'savage' and strengthens the idea that he is a threat.

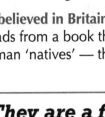
KEY QUOTE

"They are a fierce, morose, and intractable people"

This quote about Andaman natives is from one of Holmes's books. He calls the book the "latest authority" on the Andaman islands, so it's a pretty good indicator of the prejudiced views of the Victorian era.

Wealth and Greed

The novel takes a pretty dim view of wealth and greed. Love definitely wins the day — isn't that sweet.

Different characters have different views about money

1) Some characters <u>seek wealth</u> — the <u>plot</u> of the novel is <u>driven</u> by their greed:

- 'The four' stole the Agra treasure because they wanted to be "rich men".

- <u>Major Sholto</u> stole the treasure even though he was already wealthy. His "<u>cursed greed</u>" stopped him <u>sharing</u> the treasure with <u>Mary</u>.

© Chris Wooley

2) Other characters <u>don't</u> seek wealth:

- <u>Thaddeus</u> isn't greedy — he "desired no more" money, so he sent several <u>pearls</u> to Mary and wants to <u>share</u> the rest of the treasure with her.

- <u>Watson</u> views the treasure <u>negatively</u> — he worries that if Mary inherits it and becomes <u>rich</u>, he will not be able to declare his <u>love</u> for her without looking like a "<u>mere vulgar fortune-seeker</u>".

- <u>Mary</u> seems <u>indifferent</u> to the treasure — when Watson brings her the chest, she asks about it "<u>coolly enough</u>".

Theme — Love

<u>Love</u> is more <u>important</u> to Watson than wealth. When the treasure is <u>lost</u> and Watson can declare his love for Mary, he says that "Whoever had lost a treasure... I had <u>gained</u> one". Having Mary's love is more <u>valuable</u> to him than any treasure.

Wealth doesn't bring happiness

1) <u>Small</u> recognises that the Agra treasure "never brought anything but a <u>curse</u> yet upon the man who owned it". It has a <u>bad impact</u> on anyone who is involved with it.

2) The treasure causes <u>tension</u> between various characters, and it is linked to several <u>deaths</u>:

Theme — Imperialism

To a modern reader, the <u>fates</u> of the British characters who <u>stole</u> the treasure — e.g. Small's <u>imprisonment</u> and Major Sholto's <u>death</u> — may symbolise <u>justice</u> for Britain's <u>immoral exploitation</u> of its colonies.

Major Sholto and Captain Morstan

- Sholto and Morstan <u>argue</u> over how to <u>divide</u> the treasure. This results in Morstan's <u>death</u> when his weak heart is aggravated by the dispute.

- Sholto's involvement with the treasure <u>eventually</u> leads to his death <u>too</u> — he dies because he is haunted by his <u>fear</u> of Small's <u>vengeance</u>.

Thaddeus and Bartholomew Sholto

- The Sholto brothers also argue over <u>dividing</u> the treasure — Thaddeus wants to <u>share</u> it with Mary, but Bartholomew <u>doesn't</u>.

- Bartholomew <u>dies</u> after he finds the treasure — this could be a <u>moral</u> comment about the negative consequences of <u>greed</u>.

Background and Context

The treasure can be seen as a <u>symbol</u> for <u>India</u>, which was considered the '<u>jewel</u> in the crown' of the British Empire in the 19th century. Like India, the treasure is treated as a source of <u>wealth</u> and <u>power</u>, but it is also a <u>threat</u>. This contradiction reflects Victorian attitudes towards the colonies (see p.43).

KEY QUOTE

"his eyes were shining with excitement and greed"

Major Sholto could barely contain himself when Small told him about the Agra treasure. Sholto's greed plays an incredibly important role in the novel — there wouldn't be much of a story without it, really.

Love and Friendship

Here's a break from all that nasty crime and greed — except for the nasty 'friendships' further down the page.

Watson and Mary have a typical Victorian romance

1) Watson is <u>conventional</u> in his approach to love. He wants to be able to <u>provide</u> for Mary, but as an "army surgeon with a weak leg and a <u>weaker banking-account</u>", he initially doesn't think he is <u>suitable</u>.

> Watson clearly has a <u>deep love</u> for Mary — he says that her face has "neither <u>regularity</u> of feature nor <u>beauty</u> of complexion", which shows that he loves her for <u>more</u> than her appearance.

2) This situation is made <u>worse</u> by Mary's potential inheritance of the Agra <u>treasure</u> — in Victorian Britain, it was <u>unlikely</u> that a <u>rich</u> lady would marry a <u>poorer</u> man like Watson.

3) Watson only feels able to <u>declare</u> his love for Mary when they discover the treasure is <u>gone</u>.

Holmes and Watson have a fulfilling friendship

1) Although Holmes and Watson are very <u>different</u>, their personalities <u>complement</u> each other well.

2) For example, Watson's more <u>emotional</u> approach makes up for Holmes's sometimes excessive <u>rationality</u> — this is seen when Watson tries to "<u>cheer</u> and <u>amuse</u>" Mary on the drive to Thaddeus's house while Holmes rattles off <u>street names</u>.

3) They <u>both</u> get something out of their relationship:

> **Writer's Techniques — Structure**
>
> At the <u>beginning</u> and the <u>end</u> of the book, Holmes and Watson are <u>playfully arguing</u> at 221B Baker Street. While this circular structure gives <u>closure</u> to the mystery, it also <u>emphasises</u> the <u>importance</u> of their <u>friendship</u> to the story.

> <u>**Watson**</u> likes to <u>observe</u> Holmes's detective methods — it "is of the <u>greatest interest</u>" to him. He <u>admires</u> Holmes's "analytical genius" and is <u>pleased</u> to have the <u>opportunity</u> to work with him.

> <u>**Holmes**</u> has a <u>loyal</u> and <u>helpful</u> friend in Watson. Watson <u>unquestioningly</u> follows him into <u>dangerous</u> situations such as the boat chase, and Holmes can "<u>rely</u>" on him to help him with his cases.

Some relationships are destructive

1) Major Sholto and Captain Morstan had a bad influence on one another — they <u>encouraged</u> each other's <u>gambling</u> and <u>drinking</u> in the Andamans. Their friendship <u>fell apart</u> quite quickly due to <u>greed</u> and <u>betrayal</u> over the treasure.

2) Mahomet Singh, Dost Akbar, Abdullah Khan and Jonathan Small are very <u>loyal</u> to each other — they are <u>bound</u> by the treasure (see p.32). However, their loyal relationship is also destructive — it results in <u>murder</u> and leads to their <u>imprisonment</u>.

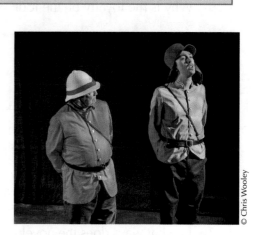

© Chris Wooley

> This reflects how many <u>white people</u> in the Victorian era saw themselves as <u>superior</u> to inhabitants of the colonies (See p.8 for more on this).

3) Tonga and Small's relationship is <u>unequal</u>. Small treats Tonga as <u>inferior</u> and exhibits him at fairs. This relationship is <u>ultimately</u> destructive for Tonga, who is <u>killed</u> while trying to escape with Small. However, it's <u>harmful</u> for <u>Small</u> too — he becomes <u>entangled</u> in Bartholomew's murder because of Tonga's actions.

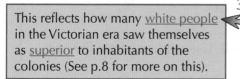

Write about the subplot of the novel...

You'll impress the examiner if you can make relevant comments on the effect of the Watson and Mary subplot. It contrasts with all the bad stuff in the main plot and emphasises what a nasty business it all was.

Practice Questions

Here we are again — the best bit. Definitely not the bit where you sigh as you turn the page because you see yet more questions that need to be answered. Remember, it's short and sweet answers for the quick questions, then we're after some longer answers (backed up with quotes and examples) for the in-depth questions. Enjoy.

Quick Questions

1) Give two things that motivate Small to commit crime.

2) How is Major Sholto punished for his wrongdoing?

3) Give one example of a forensic technique that Holmes has written about.

4) Find a quote from the novel which suggests that Holmes is:
   a) rational
   b) emotional

5) Give two examples of duality in the novel.

6) Give an example from the novel which reflects the Victorian view that the empire was:
   a) fascinating
   b) threatening

7) Name two characters in the novel who are greedy and two who are not.

8) Give one reason why Holmes and Watson's friendship is a good thing.

9) Why is the loyalty of 'the four' a bad thing as well as a good thing?

In-depth Questions

1) Explain how Small's pursuit of justice is different from Holmes's pursuit of justice.

2) How does Holmes's scientific approach make him a good detective?

3) In what ways does the novel reflect the common Victorian view of the colonies as wealthy and exotic? Give examples from the text to support your answer.

4) How does Conan Doyle emphasise the idea that greed is bad? Use evidence from the text to support your answer.

5) Briefly explain how Watson and Mary's romance conforms to Victorian conventions.

Practice Questions

I was wrong, this is actually the best bit — tasty exam questions. It might be a good idea to give some of these a go under exam conditions — the more practice you do now, the less scary writing essays will seem on exam day. If you really want to make things really tricky, try to tackle them without looking back over the section.

Exam-style Questions

1) Read the following extract from Chapter One ('The Science of Deduction'), then answer the question that follows.

> Sherlock Holmes took his bottle from the corner of the mantel-piece and his hypodermic syringe from its neat morocco case. With his long, white, nervous fingers he adjusted the delicate needle, and rolled back his left shirt-cuff. For some little time his eyes rested thoughtfully upon the sinewy forearm and wrist all dotted and scarred with innumerable puncture-marks. Finally he thrust the sharp point home, pressed down the tiny piston, and sank back into the velvet-lined arm-chair with a long sigh of satisfaction.
>
> Three times a day for many months I had witnessed this performance, but custom had not reconciled my mind to it. On the contrary, from day to day I had become more irritable at the sight, and my conscience swelled nightly within me at the thought that I had lacked the courage to protest. Again and again I had registered a vow that I should deliver my soul upon the subject, but there was that in the cool, nonchalant air of my companion which made him the last man with whom one would care to take anything approaching to a liberty. His great powers, his masterly manner, and the experience which I had had of his many extraordinary qualities, all made me diffident and backward in crossing him.
>
> Yet upon that afternoon, whether it was the Beaune which I had taken with my lunch, or the additional exasperation produced by the extreme deliberation of his manner, I suddenly felt that I could hold out no longer.
>
> "Which is it to-day?" I asked,—"morphine or cocaine?"
>
> He raised his eyes languidly from the old black-letter volume which he had opened. "It is cocaine," he said,—"a seven-per-cent solution. Would you care to try it?"
>
> "No, indeed," I answered, brusquely. "My constitution has not got over the Afghan campaign yet. I cannot afford to throw any extra strain upon it."

Explore the significance of duality in *The Sign of the Four*.
Refer to the extract and to the rest of the novel.

2) How does Conan Doyle explore ideas about friendship in the novel?

3) Read Chapter Twelve from "This is a very serious matter, Small" to "We have not heard your story, and we cannot tell how far justice may originally have been on your side".

How is the theme of crime and justice significant in the novel? Write about:
• the significance of the theme of crime and justice in this extract, and
• the significance of the theme of crime and justice in the novel as a whole.

4) Read Chapter Two from "'Au revoir,' said our visitor" to "'What do you make of this fellow's scribble?'". Explore how Conan Doyle presents ideas about emotion and rationality in this extract and in the novel as a whole.

Form, Structure and Narrative

Conan Doyle put *The Sign of the Four* together very carefully to make sure the reader is always in suspense.

'The Sign of the Four' is a serialised novel...

1) The novel has a <u>focused plot</u>. It has twelve <u>short chapters</u> that mainly follow <u>Holmes's investigation</u>. There is also a <u>subplot</u> — Mary and John's <u>romance</u> — that runs <u>alongside</u> the main action.

2) In the Victorian era, many novels were <u>serialised</u> (published in <u>instalments</u>) in <u>newspapers</u> and <u>magazines</u> — authors had to make sure the reader would want to read the <u>next instalment</u> enough to <u>buy</u> the paper. Conan Doyle encourages his readers to keep reading by creating <u>suspense</u> at the <u>end</u> of each <u>chapter</u>. For example:

> **Background and Context**
>
> *The Sign of the Four* was <u>serialised</u> in several <u>journals</u> before it was published as a separate book.

- In Chapter Three, a mysterious "piping <u>voice</u>" comes from within the <u>house</u>. This <u>cliffhanger</u> makes the reader want to find out <u>who</u> the voice belongs to.
- Chapter Eleven ends with the discovery that the <u>treasure chest</u> is <u>empty</u>. This helps to hold the reader's <u>attention</u> now that Small has been <u>captured</u>.

...and it mostly follows the form of detective fiction

Detective fiction became increasingly popular in Victorian times.

1) *The Sign of the Four* contains many <u>elements</u> of <u>detective fiction</u>:

Detective Fiction	*The Sign of the Four*
There is a <u>brilliant detective</u> and a <u>companion</u> who is <u>not as clever</u>.	Holmes solves very <u>difficult</u> cases that nobody else can. Watson is <u>less intelligent</u> and <u>perceptive</u> than Holmes.
The <u>plot</u> is normally based on a <u>central mystery</u> that must be <u>solved</u> using <u>clues</u>.	There are several <u>linked mysteries</u> in the novel that are all related to the central mystery of the <u>Agra treasure</u>.
<u>Clues</u> are <u>gradually revealed</u> to the reader throughout the story to build <u>tension</u>.	Conan Doyle increases <u>tension</u> by introducing <u>new clues</u> and pieces of <u>backstory</u> that <u>deepen</u> the central mystery.
The <u>police force</u> is often shown to be much less <u>competent</u> than the detective.	<u>Athelney Jones</u> is a <u>poor</u> detective — he arrests the <u>wrong</u> people and needs Holmes's <u>help</u> to solve the case.

2) There are also some <u>differences</u>. For example, in detective fiction, the detective usually solves the mystery at the <u>end</u> of the story. However, in *The Sign of the Four*, Holmes solves the case <u>early on</u> — there is "nothing at all <u>new</u>" to him in much of <u>Small's narrative</u> in Chapter Twelve. This emphasises Holmes's <u>skill</u>.

The novel's structure builds suspense

This structure is called Freytag's pyramid.

© ITV/REX/Shutterstock

The Sign of the Four has a <u>clear structure</u>:

1) <u>Exposition</u> — the mystery is <u>introduced</u> by Mary and Thaddeus.

2) <u>Rising Action</u> — the <u>tension builds</u> as small clues and pieces of information are <u>gradually revealed</u> to Holmes and the reader.

3) <u>Climax</u> — the <u>action builds</u> to <u>peak excitement</u> in Chapter Ten as Holmes and Watson pursue Small and Tonga down the Thames.

4) <u>Falling Action</u> — the <u>pace</u> of the action <u>slows</u> down after Small's <u>capture</u> and Tonga's <u>death</u>, and the suspense <u>lessens</u>.

5) <u>Resolution</u> — the mystery is <u>fully resolved</u> in the final chapter.

Form, Structure and Narrative

Most of the narrative is from Watson's viewpoint...

1) Watson is a <u>first-person limited narrator</u> — the story is told from Watson's <u>point of view</u>, and it only includes things that he <u>knows</u>, or things that he has <u>seen</u> or <u>heard</u> himself.

See p.26 for more on Watson as a narrator.

2) This allows Conan Doyle to maintain the novel's sense of <u>mystery</u>, as the reader <u>doesn't discover</u> anything until <u>Watson</u> does.

> The reader receives information in <u>small chunks</u> as Watson learns more about the case — the reader doesn't have access to the <u>bigger picture</u> that Holmes can see. This creates <u>suspense</u>, as it makes it <u>harder</u> for the reader to <u>predict</u> what Holmes will do <u>next</u> or what his <u>theories</u> will be.

3) Watson is an <u>audience surrogate</u> — he <u>reacts</u> to the novel's events <u>as they happen</u> in the same way that a <u>reader</u> might, and he shares the same <u>emotions</u>. This makes him easy to <u>identify</u> with.

4) Holmes often has to <u>explain</u> his <u>deductions</u> to Watson. These <u>explanations</u> make Holmes's ideas <u>clearer</u> to the reader.

© Chris Wooley

5) Watson seems to be a fairly <u>reliable narrator</u>. He reports the <u>dialogue</u> of other characters <u>in full</u> and appears to give an <u>accurate picture</u> of events.

6) However, he is not completely <u>impartial</u>. Watson's <u>opinions</u> influence the way he presents <u>other characters</u>, which influences the <u>reader's view</u> of these characters. For example:

- Watson <u>trivialises</u> Holmes's "<u>egotism</u>" and "<u>small vanity</u>", and he <u>praises</u> Holmes more than he <u>criticises</u> him in the novel.

- He views Wiggins as a "<u>disreputable</u> little scarecrow" and finds his air of "<u>superiority</u>" <u>amusing</u>, encouraging the reader to do the same.

...but other viewpoints are included too

1) Conan Doyle uses <u>embedded narratives</u> to present other characters' <u>viewpoints</u> — this gives the reader a <u>different perspective</u> on the novel's <u>events</u>.

An embedded narrative is a story that appears within another story.

Thaddeus Sholto (Chapter Four)

- Thaddeus's account of his father's <u>confession</u> and <u>death</u> solves the mystery of Captain Morstan's <u>disappearance</u> — it includes <u>Major Sholto's narrative</u>, which reveals how Captain Morstan <u>died</u>.

- However, it also introduces <u>new mysteries</u> — it's not clear <u>where</u> the <u>Agra treasure</u> came from or <u>who</u> the <u>man</u> at the window was.

Jonathan Small (Chapter Twelve)

- Small's narrative provides a <u>first-hand account</u> of the theft of the <u>Agra treasure</u>.

- This account <u>proves</u> Holmes's <u>theories</u> about the case. This makes the <u>end</u> of the novel more <u>satisfying</u> for the reader, as it shows that Holmes has been <u>right</u> all along.

2) These <u>alternative perspectives</u> are presented through <u>Watson's narration</u> — he <u>recounts</u> the <u>words</u> of Thaddeus and Small to the reader, but the reader doesn't have access to their <u>thoughts</u>. It's hard to judge how <u>reliable</u> Thaddeus and Small are as narrators and whether they are <u>holding back</u> information.

3) Thaddeus's and Small's accounts function as <u>flashbacks</u> — they reveal <u>important details</u> about <u>past events</u> to the reader at <u>key moments</u> in the plot. Thaddeus's narrative <u>adds</u> to the <u>mystery</u> of the novel, but Small's account helps to <u>resolve</u> the <u>mystery</u> surrounding the <u>treasure</u> and <u>Bartholomew's murder</u>.

EXAM TIP

Write about the novel's form...

You could mention how the inclusion of features of the gothic novel form in *The Sign of the Four*, such as mysterious settings (p.54) and the idea of 'the double' (p.42), makes it more frightening for the reader.

Language

Conan Doyle's language can seem a bit formal at times, but stick with it. *The Sign of the Four* gets a lot easier to read once you've got used to the paragraph-long sentences and looked up all those weird words.

Watson's narrative is romanticised

Background and Context

In the late 19th century, many authors used a style called <u>Realism</u>, which describes life as it <u>truly</u> is. *The Sign of the Four*'s narrative is <u>romanticised</u>, but Holmes's <u>scientific investigation</u> adds <u>realism</u>.

1) Watson's narrative contains <u>detailed descriptions</u> of <u>settings</u> and <u>characters</u> — this helps to create <u>vivid images</u>. His descriptions are often <u>romanticised</u> — he presents an <u>idealised</u> or less <u>realistic image</u> of the thing that he's describing.

2) For example, he describes Mary as having a "<u>sweet and amiable</u>" expression and "<u>spiritual and sympathetic</u>" eyes. This <u>emotive language</u> reflects Watson's <u>attraction</u> to Mary and gives the reader a <u>biased</u> view of her.

Emotive language provokes an emotional reaction in the reader.

3) Watson's descriptions of Pondicherry Lodge are <u>exaggerated</u> to emphasise the <u>drama</u> of the setting — for example, Watson says the "<u>gloom</u>" and "<u>deathly silence</u>" of Pondicherry Lodge "<u>struck a chill</u> to the <u>heart</u>". This creates a <u>tense</u> and <u>threatening</u> mood as Watson approaches the house.

There is lots of figurative language in the novel

Figurative language is a word or a phrase that isn't meant literally.

SIMILE
- Conan Doyle uses <u>similes</u> to create <u>vivid images</u>. Holmes describes a <u>cloud</u> over London that "<u>floats</u> like a pink <u>feather</u> from some gigantic flamingo" — this emphasises the cloud's <u>delicate</u> and <u>beautiful</u> appearance.
- Similes are also used to create <u>humour</u>. When <u>Toby</u> picks up the creosote scent, he is "like a <u>connoisseur</u>" smelling "<u>a famous vintage</u>". The image of a dog <u>behaving</u> like a <u>refined</u> wine-taster is <u>amusing</u>.

METAPHOR
- Watson describes the case as "<u>a labyrinth</u>" (maze) in Chapter Seven as he reflects on what they've learnt.
- This emphasises its <u>complexity</u>. In <u>Greek mythology</u>, the labyrinth was home to a <u>monster</u> called the Minotaur — the metaphor could therefore also hint at <u>danger</u> ahead.

HYPERBOLE
- Holmes uses <u>hyperbole</u> to describe Toby's ability to track the creosote trail "to the <u>world's end</u>".
- This emphasises Toby's <u>skill</u>, giving the reader <u>confidence</u> that he'll succeed.

Dialogue reflects personality

1) <u>Holmes's</u> dialogue is often <u>precise</u> and <u>unemotional</u>:

- He uses lots of <u>scientific</u> and <u>technical</u> terms, such as "hypothesis" and "hydrocarbon". This gives the reader an <u>insight</u> into his <u>logical mind</u> and shows his <u>scientific knowledge</u>.

- However, his speech is <u>more poetic</u> when he's <u>emotional</u>. In Chapter One, he describes how "<u>fog swirls</u> down the street and <u>drifts</u> across the <u>dun-coloured</u> houses" — this <u>dreary image</u> reflects his <u>melancholy mood</u>.

© THOMPSON THEATRE COLLECTION/ArenaPAL

2) In contrast, <u>Watson's</u> dialogue is often <u>emotional</u>:

- He uses lots of <u>exclamations</u>, such as "Thank God!" and "A savage!" — these <u>sudden outbursts</u> create a sense of <u>urgency</u> that highlights Watson's <u>emotional nature</u>.

- However, he also uses <u>medical terms</u>, such as "tetanus" and "pathological". This reflects his <u>medical background</u>, which reminds the reader that he has a <u>rational</u>, <u>scientific</u> side.

Language

Conan Doyle uses dialogue to show social class

1) Conan Doyle uses <u>non-standard English</u> to convey the <u>accent</u> and <u>dialect</u> of working-class characters such as Mrs Smith and Wiggins:

- <u>non-standard spellings</u> — words are spelt <u>phonetically</u> (as they would be <u>pronounced</u>). e.g. Mrs Smith says "<u>winder</u>" instead of 'window', and "<u>ain't</u>" instead of 'are not'.
- <u>omission</u> — <u>letters</u> are often left off the <u>start</u> or <u>end</u> of words, e.g. "I'd <u>ha'</u> thought <u>nothin'</u>" instead of "I'd have thought nothing".
- <u>non-standard grammar</u> — grammatical <u>errors</u> such as <u>double negatives</u> are included, e.g. "I <u>didn't</u> hear <u>no one</u> else" instead of "I didn't hear anyone else" or "I heard no one else".
- <u>terms of address</u> — <u>titles</u> are used to acknowledge the <u>superior social status</u> of others, e.g. Wiggins calls Holmes "<u>guv'nor</u>" and "<u>sir</u>", which shows he <u>recognises</u> Holmes's <u>authority</u>.

2) Characters from <u>higher</u> social classes (e.g. Holmes, Watson and Mary) use <u>formal language</u>. Their dialogue contains <u>formal sentence structures</u>, such as "if I should see anything of the Aurora I shall let him know that you are uneasy".

© ITV/REX/Shutterstock

Character — Tonga

Tonga has <u>no dialogue</u> in the novel. This makes him seem more <u>animalistic</u>, which reinforces his status as a '<u>savage</u>' (see p.8) and a <u>foreigner</u> who is <u>not part</u> of British society.

Conan Doyle uses irony to create humour

<u>Irony</u> is when a writer says the <u>opposite</u> of what they <u>really mean</u>, or points out the <u>difference</u> between how things <u>seem</u> and how they actually <u>are</u>. Conan Doyle <u>mainly</u> uses irony in *The Sign of the Four* to highlight the <u>failings</u> of the <u>police force</u>:

1) In Chapter Six, Jones <u>criticises</u> Holmes for valuing "mere <u>theories</u>" over "<u>Facts</u>", then arrests Thaddeus <u>without any evidence</u> of his guilt.

> This is <u>ironic</u> because Jones does <u>exactly</u> what he accuses Holmes of doing — he trusts in <u>his theory</u> too much and ignores the <u>facts</u>. This makes Jones look <u>foolish</u>.

2) In Chapter Nine, Watson makes the <u>ironic comment</u> that Jones was a "<u>masterful</u> professor of <u>common sense</u>" at Pondicherry Lodge.

> Watson <u>really</u> means the <u>opposite</u> — Jones <u>ignored</u> all common sense. This emphasises Jones's <u>incompetence</u>.

Background and Context

Conan Doyle's use of irony is <u>funny</u>, but he is also making a <u>serious point</u> about the <u>ineffectiveness</u> of London's <u>police detectives</u>. *The Sign of the Four* was published in <u>1890</u>, a few years after the Metropolitan Police <u>failed to catch</u> a notorious murderer, <u>Jack the Ripper</u> (see p.6).

3) Holmes often makes <u>sarcastic comments</u> about the "accredited representatives of the law" — their <u>skills</u> don't match up to their <u>official status</u>.

4) These comments highlight an <u>ironic situation</u> in the novel — the supposed '<u>experts</u>' (the police) are <u>useless</u> at detection, so the <u>amateur</u> "unofficial" detective (Holmes) is the only person who can <u>solve</u> the case.

"all this came out in a wild whirl of words"

Watson often describes how characters behave when they speak. Small expresses himself in a "wild whirl of words" when he explains why he deserves the treasure, which suggests he's speaking passionately.

Symbolism and Imagery

Conan Doyle packs lots of symbolism into *The Sign of the Four* to help him hammer home important ideas. He also uses loads of imagery to bring Victorian London to life in all its soggy, industrial glory. Delightful.

The Agra treasure symbolises the destructive nature of wealth

> The Agra treasure is a motif (recurring symbol). Conan Doyle uses it to explore ideas about wealth.

1) Many characters want to possess the treasure, but it doesn't bring them happiness. Small is imprisoned twice and Captain Morstan, Major Sholto and Bartholomew Sholto all die because of the treasure — this symbolises the destructive impact of desire for wealth.

2) The treasure is also an "impassable barrier" that separates Watson from Mary — it prevents him from asking her to marry him. Watson and Mary's happiness is only secured when the treasure is lost.

3) The story of the Agra treasure is a microcosm of British imperialism:

© Chris Wooley

- The treasure is removed from India by a corrupt British official (Major Sholto), even though he has no right to it.
- The theft of the treasure symbolises Britain's exploitation of the empire's resources in the 19th century — see p.8.

> A microcosm is a smaller representation of something else.

'The sign of the four' motif adds to the mystery

1) Another key motif is the phrase "the sign of the four", which appears on pieces of paper throughout the novel, sometimes alongside a "curious hieroglyphic".

> 'the four' are the four men who stole the Agra treasure from the Rajah.

2) This motif appears early in the plot — Holmes finds the phrase on or close to the dead bodies of Major Sholto and Bartholomew Sholto, so the reader knows that it is significant. However, its meaning is not explained until the last chapter. This makes it seem more mysterious and threatening.

3) The phrase symbolises the agreement between 'the four' that they should "each always act for all".

Weapons also have symbolic meaning

1) Holmes carries a revolver, and Watson has a "service-revolver" from his time in the army. The revolver was a typical western gun in the 19th century — it symbolises western power and military might.

2) In contrast, Tonga uses primitive weapons — he shoots "murderous darts" tipped with poison from a blowpipe. This symbolises what Victorians would have seen as Tonga's 'uncivilised' nature — they link him to Small's description of the "wild cannibal natives" of the Andaman Islands who use "poisoned darts".

3) In Chapter Ten, the poisoned dart that Tonga blows at Watson and Holmes misses, leaving them unharmed. Tonga is quickly killed after Holmes and Watson shoot him with their revolvers.

- This exchange symbolises the conflict between Britain and 'hostile' natives in the Empire — the effectiveness of the revolver against Tonga symbolises Britain's superior military power.
- Watson describes the "horrible death" that "passed so close" to them when Tonga fired his dart. This reflects the Victorian fear that people from the colonies posed a threat to the security of the British Empire.

Symbolism and Imagery

Imagery of weather is used to create atmosphere

The <u>weather</u> at different times and places affects the novel's <u>mood</u>:

1) In Chapter Three, Conan Doyle uses <u>pathetic fallacy</u> to describe the "Mud-coloured clouds" that "<u>drooped sadly</u>" over London's streets. The clouds acting "sadly" creates a <u>gloomy</u> mood, which adds to the <u>suspense</u> as Holmes, Watson and Mary travel to the theatre.

> Personification means describing a non-living thing as though it's human. Pathetic fallacy means giving human emotions to nature to create a mood.

2) At <u>Pondicherry Lodge</u>, there are "<u>heavy clouds</u>" in the sky, but the <u>moon</u> is "<u>peeping</u>" through. This <u>personification</u> of the moon as being able to <u>see</u> through the <u>clearing clouds</u> hints that some of the mystery is about be <u>solved</u>. This creates an <u>expectant mood</u>.

3) In Chapter Seven, Holmes points out how the "red rim of the sun pushes itself over the London cloud-bank". This image of <u>sunrise</u> reflects the mood of <u>hope</u> that is created by the discovery of the "palpable clue" of the <u>creosote trail</u>.

> **Character — Sherlock Holmes**
>
> Holmes's language is <u>romanticised</u> and <u>poetic</u> here, which is <u>unusual</u> for him. It emphasises how <u>positive</u> he feels now that he is pursuing an <u>unusual case</u>.

Images of light and dark symbolise opposites

1) <u>Darkness</u> often symbolises <u>mystery</u> and <u>uncertainty</u>:

- On the way to Thaddeus's house, Watson describes the "<u>gloom</u>" of London's streets, and Thaddeus's street is "<u>dark</u>". This darkness symbolises Holmes's lack of <u>clarity</u> about Mary's case at this point.
- Watson describes Pondicherry Lodge as a "great <u>black house</u>" that's overshadowed by "<u>black tragedy</u>" — this symbolises the <u>dark mystery</u> that surrounds the <u>house</u> and the <u>Sholto family</u>.

© Photo 12 / Alamy Stock Photo

2) In contrast, <u>light</u> is often used to symbolise <u>clarity</u>:

- As Toby follows the <u>creosote scent</u> in Chapter Seven, the countryside is bathed in a "cold <u>grey light</u>" — this <u>muted light</u> symbolises the <u>partial understanding</u> of the case that Holmes has gained so far.
- In Chapter Ten, a <u>lantern</u> throws "a long, flickering <u>funnel of light</u>" in front of the <u>police boat</u> as it chases the Aurora. This symbolises Holmes's pursuit of the <u>truth</u>, which is bringing <u>clarity</u> to the case.

3) Light and dark are also used to symbolise <u>good</u> and <u>bad</u>. In Chapter Seven, Mary is <u>bathed</u> in light "<u>shining</u> through stained glass", which makes her seem <u>angelic</u>. In contrast, Tonga is often associated with <u>darkness</u> — he's described as a "<u>dark mass</u>" just before he tries to <u>kill</u> Holmes and Watson.

4) Images of <u>light</u> in dark places often <u>foreshadow</u> the discovery of <u>new information</u>:

- The <u>darkness</u> of Thaddeus's street is <u>broken</u> by a "<u>glimmer</u>" in his window. This hints that his story will throw some <u>light</u> on the case.
- Before Bartholomew's <u>body</u> is discovered, a "<u>moonbeam</u>" is reflected from the "<u>garret</u> window". This puts a <u>spotlight</u> on the location of <u>Bartholomew's body</u>.

> Foreshadowing is when an author hints at a future event.

KEY QUOTE

"a dense drizzly fog lay low upon the great city."

Conan Doyle uses imagery like this to maintain a mysterious atmosphere in the novel — the image of a thick wall of fog adds to the mood of threat and secrecy by suggesting that it is smothering the city.

Setting

Now for a page where London and India compete for the award for 'Most Dismal Setting in a Novel Ever'.

London has a mysterious and threatening atmosphere

1) London is often presented as <u>foggy</u> and <u>dark</u> in the novel. Watson mentions London's "<u>damp fog</u>", and Holmes describes it as a "<u>dreary</u>" place that's shrouded in "<u>yellow fog</u>".

2) The city is presented as particularly <u>gloomy</u> and <u>threatening</u> on the journey to Thaddeus Sholto's house:

- The city is <u>covered</u> in a "<u>dense drizzly fog</u>", and the air is "<u>steamy</u>" and "<u>vaporous</u>". The streets are <u>hidden</u> from view, which suggests that they are places of <u>secrecy</u>.

- The characters travel through "<u>tortuous</u> by-streets", a "<u>labyrinth</u> of streets" and "<u>interminable</u> lines" of terraces. This makes London seem <u>confusing</u> and <u>oppressive</u>.

- Conan Doyle describes the lines of terraced houses as "<u>monster tentacles</u>" that the "<u>giant</u> city was <u>throwing out</u>" — this makes London seem like a <u>fearsome</u> creature.

> These descriptions of endless streets reflect London's rapid expansion in the 19th century (see p.6).

3) This presentation reflects the <u>uncertainty</u> around the case early in the novel. Setting the novel in a place that would have been <u>familiar</u> to many readers adds to the <u>tension</u>, as it makes the story more <u>believable</u>.

Individual houses represent their inhabitants

Thaddeus's apartment is unusual

- It seems <u>out of place</u> in London, which reflects Thaddeus's <u>eccentric nature</u>.

- The apartment has a "suggestion of <u>Eastern luxury</u>". This shows Thaddeus has been influenced by his family's time in <u>India</u>.

Pondicherry Lodge is dark and fortified

- The house is "<u>black</u>" and "plunged in <u>shadow</u>". This reflects Major Sholto's <u>immorality</u>.

- The grounds are <u>surrounded</u> by a "high stone wall", which reflects Major Sholto's <u>secrecy</u> and <u>selfish desire</u> to hide the treasure.

The novel's past events are mainly set in India

1) The <u>exotic</u> setting of India adds to the air of <u>mystery</u>. Small describes the "<u>fire</u> and <u>blood</u>" of India during the 1857 rebellion (see p.8) — this image of <u>heat</u> and <u>chaos</u> contrasts with the <u>gloomy</u> London settings and makes India seem more <u>foreign</u>.

> Travel was much more difficult and less common in the 19th century than it is today, so India would have seemed more exotic to a Victorian reader than it does to a modern reader.

© Chris Wooley

2) Conan Doyle <u>presents</u> India as a <u>dangerous</u> place:

- Small says that the <u>Indian</u> city of Agra is full of "<u>fierce</u> devil-worshippers" and "black <u>fiends</u>". These <u>racist</u> descriptions reflect the <u>stereotypical</u> Victorian idea that foreigners were <u>savage</u> and <u>dangerous</u>, which makes India seem <u>uncivilised</u>.

- Small describes the <u>Andaman Islands</u> as "<u>fever-stricken</u>" and "<u>infested</u> with <u>wild</u> cannibal natives". This constant threat of <u>illness</u> and <u>violence</u> makes it seem like a <u>hostile</u> place.

EXAM TIP

Link the novel's settings to its context...

On the Thames in Chapter Ten, Holmes and the others encounter "barges, steamers, merchant-vessels". This bustling night scene reflects the industrial and commercial nature of Victorian London.

Practice Questions

Just as you triumphantly approach the end of this enlightening section, something dreadful slithers into view like an inconvenient monster. Sorry about that — just practising my writing techniques. I've no idea why all those publishers rejected me. Anyway... where were we? Ah yes, another page of practice questions. As usual, write a few words or a sentence for the quick questions, and a paragraph or so for the in-depth ones.

Quick Questions

1) Give two examples of cliffhangers in the novel. Why does Conan Doyle use cliffhangers?

2) Give two features of the detective fiction form that Conan Doyle uses in the novel.

3) Which of the following sentences is correct?
   a) Watson's narrative is limited because he doesn't tell the reader everything that he knows.
   b) Watson's narrative is limited because he can only tell the reader what he knows.

4) Which of the following best describes Holmes's dialogue?
   a) passionate and dramatic   b) clear-minded and clever   c) cruel and aggressive

5) Give three ways in which Conan Doyle uses dialogue to make his working-class characters more realistic.

6) What does 'the sign of the four' motif symbolise?

7) What does fog symbolise in the novel?

8) Give an example from the novel of imagery that helps to create an ominous mood.

9) Write a sentence that explains one key difference between the settings of India and London.

In-depth Questions

1) Give one way that the form of *The Sign of the Four* is different from detective fiction. Why do you think Conan Doyle chose to make this change?

2) How does Watson's view of Holmes influence the reader's impression of Holmes? Use evidence from the text to explain your answer.

3) Find an example in Chapter Two where Watson uses romanticised language. Explain the effect of this language on the reader. Use quotes from the text to support your answer.

4) In your own words, explain why Victorian readers might have found Conan Doyle's presentation of India frightening.

Practice Questions

And now for another round of exam-style questions (do a little cheer — it'll make you feel better). Some of these questions are quite tricky, but tackling them now will make the exam seem a lot less scary. Think of this page as a dress rehearsal — it's a good chance to iron out any issues you might be having before the big day.

Exam-style Questions

1) Read this extract from Chapter Ten ('The End of the Islander'), then answer the question that follows.

> We were not more than four boat's lengths behind them, both boats flying at a tremendous pace. It was a clear reach of the river, with Barking Level upon one side and the melancholy Plumstead Marshes upon the other. At our hail the man in the stern sprang up from the deck and shook his two clinched fists at us, cursing the while in a high, cracked voice. He was a good-sized, powerful man, and as he stood poising himself with his legs astride I could see that from the thigh downwards there was but a wooden stump upon the right side. At the sound of his strident, angry cries there was movement in the huddled bundle upon the deck. It straightened itself into a little black man — the smallest I have ever seen — with a great, misshapen head and a shock of tangled, dishevelled hair. Holmes had already drawn his revolver, and I whipped out mine at the sight of this savage, distorted creature. He was wrapped in some sort of dark ulster or blanket, which left only his face exposed; but that face was enough to give a man a sleepless night. Never have I seen features so deeply marked with all bestiality and cruelty. His small eyes glowed and burned with a sombre light, and his thick lips writhed back from his teeth, which grinned and chattered at us with a half animal fury.
>
> "Fire if he raises his hand," said Holmes, quietly. We were within a boat's-length by this time, and almost within touch of our quarry. I can see the two of them now as they stood, the white man with his legs far apart, shrieking out curses, and the unhallowed dwarf with his hideous face, and his strong yellow teeth gnashing at us in the light of our lantern.
>
> It was well that we had so clear a view of him. Even as we looked he plucked out from under his covering a short, round piece of wood, like a school-ruler, and clapped it to his lips. Our pistols rang out together. He whirled round, threw up his arms, and with a kind of choking cough fell sideways into the stream.

How does Conan Doyle create a sense of danger in *The Sign of the Four*?
Refer to the extract and to the rest of the novel.

2) Read Chapter Eight from "He stretched his hand up" to "Jonathan Small would give a good deal not to have employed him". How does Conan Doyle present the theme of imperialism in this extract and in the novel as a whole?
Write about:
   • how Conan Doyle uses symbolism to present the theme of imperialism
   • other techniques he uses to present the theme of imperialism.

3) Explain the importance of Watson's narrative voice in *The Sign of the Four*.

4) Read Chapter Four ('The Story of the Bald-Headed Man') from the start of the chapter to "As it burned it filled the air with a subtle and aromatic odour." Explore the effects of Conan Doyle's use of imagery in this extract and in the rest of the novel.

Exam Preparation

Getting to know the text will put you at a massive advantage in the exam. It's not enough just to read it though — you've got to get to grips with the nitty-gritty bits. It's all about gathering evidence...

The exam questions will test four main skills

You will need to show the examiner that you can:

1) Write about the text in a <u>thoughtful way</u> — <u>picking out</u> appropriate <u>examples</u> and <u>quotations</u> to back up your opinions.

2) <u>Identify</u> and <u>explain</u> features of the text's <u>form</u>, <u>structure</u> and <u>language</u>. Show how the author uses these to create <u>meanings</u> and <u>effects</u>.

3) Relate the text to its <u>cultural, social and historical background</u>.

4) Write in a <u>clear</u>, <u>well-structured</u> way. <u>5%</u> of the marks in your English Literature exams are for <u>spelling</u>, <u>punctuation</u> and <u>grammar</u>. Make sure that your writing is as <u>accurate</u> as possible.

Preparation is important

1) It's <u>important</u> to cover <u>all</u> the <u>different sections</u> of this book in your <u>revision</u>. You need to make sure you <u>understand</u> the text's <u>context</u>, <u>plot</u>, <u>characters</u>, <u>themes</u> and <u>writer's techniques</u>.

2) In the <u>exam</u>, you'll need to <u>bring together</u> your <u>ideas</u> about these topics to answer the question <u>quickly</u>.

3) Think about the different <u>characters</u> and <u>themes</u> in the text, and write down some <u>key points</u> and <u>ideas</u> about each one. Then, find some <u>evidence</u> to support each point — this could be something from <u>any</u> of the <u>sections</u> in this book. You could set out your evidence in a <u>table</u> like this:

Theme: Crime and Justice	
Motives for crime	Greed — theft of Agra treasure by 'the four' and Major Sholto. Revenge — Small's "overpowering" desire to kill Major Sholto. Loyalty — Tonga's murder of Bartholomew Sholto.
Legal justice	Some characters escape legal justice, e.g. Major Sholto. Others cannot escape, e.g. Small. Links to class and wealth.
Personal justice	Small believes he has "earned the Agra treasure", and he regards his theft of it from Bartholomew as justice.
Role of police	Shown to be inept through wrongful arrest of Thaddeus — reflects popular conception of police in late 19th-century Britain.
Irony	Only Holmes (the amateur detective) can bring about legal justice — reinforces incompetence of police.

Preparing to succeed — a cunning plot indeed...

Knowing the plot inside out will be unbelievably helpful in the exam. It'll help you to stay calm and make sure you write a brilliant answer that positively glitters with little gems of evidence. The exam's just a chance for you to show off...

The Exam Question

This page deals with how to approach an exam question. The stuff below will help you get started on a scorching exam answer, more scorching than, say, a phoenix cooking fiery fajitas in a flaming furnace.

Read the question carefully and underline key words

1) The style of question you'll get depends on which <u>exam board</u> you're taking.

2) Read all the <u>instructions</u> carefully. Make sure you know <u>how many</u> questions you need to answer and <u>how much time</u> you should spend answering each one.

3) If the question has <u>more than one part</u>, look at the total number of marks for each bit. This should help you to plan your <u>time</u> in the exam.

4) <u>Read</u> the question at least <u>twice</u> so you completely understand it. <u>Underline</u> the key words. If you're given an <u>extract</u>, underline <u>important</u> words or phrases in that too.

Henry didn't read the weather report carefully enough when planning his weekend activities.

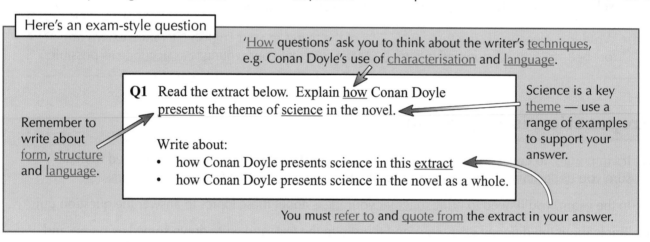

Here's an exam-style question

'<u>How</u> questions' ask you to think about the writer's <u>techniques</u>, e.g. Conan Doyle's use of <u>characterisation</u> and <u>language</u>.

Q1 Read the extract below. Explain <u>how</u> Conan Doyle <u>presents</u> the theme of <u>science</u> in the novel.

Write about:
- how Conan Doyle presents science in this <u>extract</u>
- how Conan Doyle presents science in the novel as a whole.

Remember to write about <u>form</u>, <u>structure</u> and <u>language</u>.

Science is a key <u>theme</u> — use a range of examples to support your answer.

You must <u>refer to</u> and <u>quote from</u> the extract in your answer.

Get to know exam language

Some <u>words</u> come up time and again in <u>exam questions</u>. Have a look at some <u>specimen</u> questions, pick out words that are <u>often used</u> in questions and make sure that you <u>understand</u> what they mean. You could <u>write a few down</u> whilst you're revising. For example:

Question Word	You need to...
Explore / Explain	Show <u>how</u> the writer deals with a <u>theme</u>, <u>character</u> or <u>idea</u>. Make several <u>different</u> points to answer the question.
How does	Think about the <u>techniques</u> or <u>literary features</u> that the author uses to get their point across.
Give examples	Use <u>direct quotes</u> and describe <u>events</u> from the text in your own words.
Refer to	Read the question so that you know if you need to write about just an <u>extract</u>, or an extract and the <u>rest of the text</u>.

The advice squad — the best cops in the NYPD...

Whatever question you're asked in the exam, your answer should touch on the main characters, themes, structure and language of the text. All the stuff we've covered in the rest of the book in fact. It's so neat, it's almost like we planned it.

Planning Your Answer

I'll say this once — and then I'll probably repeat it several times — it is absolutely, completely, totally and utterly essential that you make a plan before you start writing. Only a fool jumps right in without a plan...

Plan your answer before you start

1) If you plan, you're less likely to forget something <u>important</u>.

2) A good plan will help you <u>organise</u> your ideas — and write a good, <u>well-structured</u> essay.

3) Write your plan at the <u>top of your answer booklet</u> and draw a <u>neat line</u> through it when you've finished.

4) <u>Don't</u> spend <u>too long</u> on your plan. It's only <u>rough work</u>, so you don't need to write in full sentences. Here are a few <u>examples</u> of different ways you can plan your answer:

Introduction
An idea
Conclusion ── Spider diagram
Another idea
Another idea

Bullet points...
- Introduction...
- An idea...
- The next idea...
- Another idea...
- Yet another idea...
- Conclusion...

Include bits of evidence in your plan

1) <u>Writing</u> your essay will be much <u>easier</u> if you include <u>important quotes</u> and <u>examples</u> in your plan.

2) You could include them in a <u>table</u> like this one:

3) <u>Don't</u> spend <u>too long</u> writing out quotes though. It's just to make sure you <u>don't forget</u> anything when you write your answer.

A point...	Quote to back this up...
Another point...	Quote...
A different point...	Example...
A brand new point...	Quote...

Structure your answer

Introduction
↓
Middle Section
— paragraphs
expanding
your
argument.
↓
Conclusion

1) Your <u>introduction</u> should give a brief answer to the question you're writing about. Make it clear how you're going to <u>tackle the topic</u>.

2) The <u>middle section</u> of your essay should explain your answer in detail and give evidence to back it up. Write a <u>paragraph</u> for each point you make. Make sure you <u>comment</u> on your evidence and <u>explain how</u> it helps to <u>prove</u> your point.

3) Remember to write a <u>conclusion</u> — a paragraph at the end which <u>sums up</u> your <u>main points</u>. There's <u>more</u> about introductions and conclusions on the <u>next page</u>.

Dirk finally felt ready to tackle the topic.

To plan or not to plan, that is the question...

The answer is yes, yes, a thousand times yes. Often students dive right in, worried that planning will take up valuable time. But 5 minutes spent organising a well-structured answer is loads better than pages of waffle. Mmm waffles.

Writing Introductions and Conclusions

Now you've made that plan that I was banging on about on the last page, you'll know what your main points are. This is going to make writing your introduction and conclusion as easy as pie.

Get to the point straight away in your introduction

1) First, you need to work out what the question is asking you to do:

> How is the character of Mary Morstan important to the novel?
>
> The question is asking you to think about the role of Mary Morstan in the novel.
> Plan your essay by thinking about how this character links to the novel's plot and main themes.

2) When you've planned your essay, you should begin by giving a clear answer to the question in a sentence or two. Use the rest of the introduction to develop this idea. Try to include the main paragraph ideas that you have listed in your plan, but save the evidence for later.

3) You could also use the introduction to give your opinion. Whatever you do, make sure your introduction makes it clear how your answer fits the question.

Your conclusion must answer the question

1) The most important thing you have to do at the end of your writing is to summarise your answer to the question.

2) It's your last chance to persuade the examiner, so make your main point again.

3) Use your last sentence to really impress the examiner — it will make your essay stand out. You could develop your own opinion of the text or highlight which of your points you thought was the most interesting.

The examiner was struggling to see the answer clearly.

Use the question words in your introduction and conclusion

1) Try to use words or phrases from the question in your introduction and conclusion.

> How does Conan Doyle present wealth in the extract and in the novel as a whole?

2) This will show the examiner that you're answering the question.

> In 'The Sign of the Four', Conan Doyle presents wealth as something that many characters aspire to have, but that does not bring happiness to those who possess it.

The first line of the introduction gives a clear answer, which will lead on to the rest of the essay.

3) This will also help you keep the question fresh in your mind so your answer doesn't wander off-topic.

I've come to the conclusion that I really like pie...

To conclude, the introduction eases the examiner in gently, whilst the conclusion is your last chance to impress. But remember — the examiner doesn't want to see any new points lurking in those closing sentences.

Writing Main Paragraphs

So we've covered the beginning and the end, now it's time for the meaty bit. The roast beef in between the prawn cocktail and the treacle tart. This page is about how to structure your paragraphs. It's quite simple...

P.E.E.D. is how to put your argument together

Remember to start a new paragraph every time you make a new point.

1) P.E.E.D. stands for: Point, Example, Explain, Develop.

2) Begin each paragraph by making a point. Then give an example from the text (either a quote or a description). Next, explain how your example backs up your point.

3) Finally, try to develop your point by writing about its effect on the reader, how it links to another part of the text or what the writer's intention is in including it.

Use short quotes to support your ideas

1) Don't just use words from the novel to repeat what you've already said...

> Major Sholto's greed stops him from giving any treasure to Mary: "The cursed greed which has been my besetting sin through life has withheld from her the treasure".

This just gives an example from the text without offering any explanation or analysis.

2) Instead, it's much better to use short quotes as evidence to support a point you're making.

3) It makes the essay structure clearer and smoother if most quotes are embedded in your sentences.

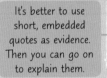

It's better to use short, embedded quotes as evidence. Then you can go on to explain them.

> Major Sholto describes the "greed" that prevents him from sharing the treasure as "cursed". This suggests that he views his desire for riches as having an almost supernatural power to cause harm to himself and others.

Get to know some literary language

1) Using literary terms in your answer will make your essay stand out — as long as you use them correctly.

2) When you're revising, think about literary terms that are relevant to the text and how you might include them in an essay. Take a look at the table below for some examples.

Literary Term	Definition	Example
Metaphor	Describing something by saying it is something else.	"the golden barrier was gone from between us"
Simile	Compares one thing to another, often using 'like' and 'as'.	"The muscles are as hard as a board"
Narrative irony	When words are used to imply the opposite of what they normally mean.	"Mr. Athelney Jones... with all his well-known energy and sagacity."

This page is so exciting — I nearly...

Now now, let's all be grown-ups and avoid the obvious joke. It's a good way of remembering how to structure your paragraphs though. Point, Example, Explain, Develop. Simple. Maybe we could make a rap or something... anyone?

In the Exam

Keeping cool in the exam can be tricky. But if you take in all the stuff on this page, you'll soon have it down to a fine art. Then you can stroll out of that exam hall with the swagger of an essay-writing master.

Don't panic if you make a mistake

1) Okay, so say you've timed the exam beautifully. Instead of putting your feet up on the desk for the last 5 minutes, it's a good idea to <u>read through</u> your <u>answers</u> and <u>correct any mistakes</u>...

2) If you want to get rid of a mistake, <u>cross it out</u>. <u>Don't scribble</u> it out as this can look messy. Make any corrections <u>neatly</u> and <u>clearly</u> instead of writing on top of the words you've already written.

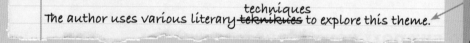

The author uses various literary ~~teknikues~~ techniques to explore this theme.

This is the clearest way to correct a mistake. Don't be tempted to try writing on top of the original word.

3) If you've <u>left out</u> a <u>word</u> or a <u>phrase</u> and you've got space to add it in <u>above</u> the line it's missing from, write the missing bit above the line with a '∧' to show exactly where it should go.

Re-read the sentence carefully to work out where the '∧' symbol needs to go.

The writer uses imagery to draw attention to this point. and hyperbole

4) If you've left out whole <u>sentences</u> or <u>paragraphs</u>, write them in a <u>separate section</u> at the <u>end</u> of the essay. Put a <u>star</u> (*) next to both the <u>extra writing</u> and the <u>place</u> you want it to go.

Always keep an eye on the time

1) It's surprisingly <u>easy</u> to <u>run out of time</u> in exams. You've got to leave <u>enough time</u> to answer <u>all</u> the questions you're asked to do. You've also got to leave enough time to <u>finish</u> each essay properly — with a <u>clear ending</u>.

2) Here are some <u>tips</u> on how to <u>avoid</u> running out of time:

- Work out <u>how much time</u> you have for each part of your answer <u>before</u> you <u>start</u>.

- Take off a few minutes at the beginning to <u>plan</u>, and a <u>few minutes</u> at the end for your <u>conclusion</u>.

- Make sure you have a <u>watch</u> to <u>time yourself</u> — and keep checking it.

- Be <u>strict</u> with yourself — if you spend <u>too long</u> on one part of your answer, you may run out of time.

- If you're <u>running out of time</u>, keep <u>calm</u>, <u>finish</u> the <u>point</u> you're on and move on to your <u>conclusion</u>.

Stephanie never had a problem with keeping cool.

Treat an exam like a spa day — just relax...

Some people actually do lose the plot when they get into the exam. The trick is to keep calm and well... carry on. If you make sure you get your exam technique sorted, you'll be as relaxed as a sloth in a room full of easy chairs.

Sample Exam Question

And now the bit you've all been waiting for — a sample exam question and a lovely little plan.
Go and make yourself a cup of tea, then settle down and enjoy.

Here's a sample exam question...

In the exam, you'll be given the full extract in the exam paper.

Read this feisty exam question. That's the best way to start...

Read the question carefully. Underline the important bits.

Write about context — e.g. how scientific developments influenced Conan Doyle's presentation of Holmes.

> Q1 Read Chapter Six ('Sherlock Holmes Gives a Demonstration') from the start of the chapter to "'It is absolutely impossible,' I answered."
>
> Write about how Conan Doyle presents Sherlock Holmes as a logical character in the extract and elsewhere in the novel.

Think about how Conan Doyle uses language to present the character of Sherlock Holmes.

You need to think about what it is that makes Holmes seem logical, e.g. his actions, his dialogue and the way other characters react to him.

You'll need to discuss the extract given in detail, but you also need to refer to the rest of the novel.

Here's how you could plan your answer

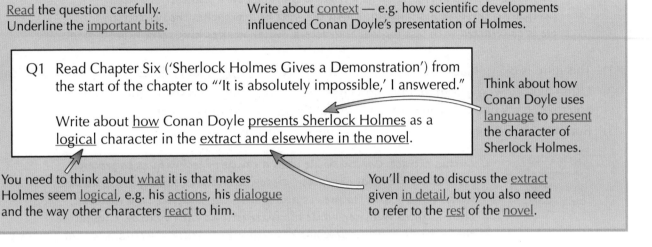

Forensic analysis of footprints

Expert; examines evidence in a "clinical" manner

Rhetorical questions & short sentences in extract

Novel's resolution shows Holmes's theories correct — logical approach effective

Context: Dr Joseph Bell — Conan Doyle's inspiration

"clinical professor"

Clear explanation of methods / thought process

Detective novel form — building evidence / finding new clues

Detective novel form and structure

Scientific language & explanations

Language: logical and scientific

Watson's narrative viewpoint

Introduction

Form and structure

Contrast with others

Holmes as a logical character

Watson admires Holmes's "marvellous faculty" for logic, so stresses this quality

Conclusion

Contrast with other characters

Reflected in form, structure, language and relationships

Holmes characterised by use of logic

Watson — more emotional, emphasises Holmes's logical nature

Context: limited use of new forensic techniques; police incompetence

Jones — doesn't apply logic; jumps to wrong conclusions

Watson and Jones contrast with Holmes

Holmes too logical — at expense of others' feelings

What do examiners eat? Why, egg-sam-wiches of course...

The most important thing to remember is DON'T PANIC. Take a deep breath, read the question, read it again, write a plan... take another deep breath... and start writing. Leave a few minutes at the end to check your answer too.

Worked Answer

These pages will show you how to take an OK answer and turn it into a really good one that will impress the examiner.

Use your introduction to get off to a good start

> These pages are all about how to word your sentences to impress the examiner, so we haven't included everything from the plan on p.63.

You might start with something like...

> Sherlock Holmes is presented as a logical character in a number of ways, including through his language and the way he approaches the mystery. He is contrasted with less logical characters, which makes him seem more logical.

1) This intro is <u>okay</u>. It acknowledges that there are <u>various ways</u> that Holmes is shown to be logical.

2) Using the <u>key words</u> from the question gives your essay <u>focus</u>, and shows the examiner you're on <u>track</u> and that you're thinking about the question from the start.

3) But there's still room for <u>improvement</u> — here's a better introduction...

This is a clear opening line that links to the question.

> In this extract, Conan Doyle uses a range of techniques to present Holmes as a logical character. Descriptions and dialogue are used to make it clear that Holmes is analysing the evidence in a rational, clear-sighted manner, while his interactions with Watson emphasise that his use of deduction has enabled him to reach conclusions that the less logical Watson cannot. Holmes's status as a highly logical 'master detective' is confirmed throughout the novel by his resolution of the mystery, the contrast between him and other characters, and his similarities to other detectives within the context of detective fiction.

This makes it clear that the essay will discuss the novel's form and context.

Develop each point with detailed comments and quotes

> Conan Doyle uses language to show Holmes's logic. Holmes uses questions and short sentences. Watson describes him as a "clinical professor", which shows Holmes is very logical.

1) This paragraph makes lots of <u>points</u> about the language in the extract. But it doesn't <u>develop</u> the points <u>fully</u> or give details about <u>how</u> the language demonstrates Holmes's logic.

2) You should develop your points with <u>detail</u> and comments:

This makes a relevant point about the extract, and then goes on to give more detail.

This explains the point by considering the effect of Holmes's language on the reader.

> The language that Holmes uses in the extract emphasises the logic of his thought processes. As he analyses the evidence surrounding Bartholomew's murder, he uses a series of short, incomplete sentences, such as "No water-pipe near.", which emphasise his rapid train of thought. The lack of any redundant words (such as 'There is...') gives the impression that Holmes is mentally composing concise, scientific notes, which reinforces the logical, orderly way in which his mind functions. Holmes's use of small details or absences to eliminate options reminds the reader of the correct conclusions that Holmes previously drew from such minute details as the scratches on Watson's watch, emphasising the validity of his logical approach.

This shows that you've thought about other parts of the novel, not just the passage given in the question.

Remember to back up your points with quotes or examples from the novel.

Worked Answer

Link your points to the novel's context and themes

1) Here's a point you could make about the way that Holmes is presented in the novel:

> Holmes is presented as logical through comparisons with other characters. Jones is described as having "occasional glimmerings of reason", providing a marked contrast to Holmes's consistent logic.

2) This paragraph <u>builds</u> on the idea that other characters' lack of logic emphasises Holmes's logical character.

3) However, you can improve it by discussing <u>how</u> this relates to the <u>themes</u> of the novel:

> Conan Doyle draws a comparison between Holmes and Jones to emphasise Holmes's logical approach. Jones takes the fact that Thaddeus Sholto is "not attractive" as proof of his guilt, an irrational claim that contrasts with Holmes's approach of "measuring, comparing, examining" to reach a valid hypothesis. Jones unscientifically tries to bend the facts to fit his theory, whereas Holmes develops a logical theory that incorporates all the facts. This contrast reinforces the idea that Holmes is a logical character by emphasising that his methods are based on scientific principles rather than guesswork.

> It's a good idea to show the examiner you're aware of how characters link to the themes of the novel (e.g. science).

> Don't forget to explain how your points link to the exam question.

4) You could develop this by focusing on the <u>context</u> in which the novel was written:

> Make sure your comments on context are linked closely to the text and the question.

> Holmes is shown to employ forensic techniques, such as the examination of footprints, that were relatively new in the 19th century. These techniques would have been unfamiliar to many Victorian readers, making Holmes's methods seem more scientific and logical than they do to modern readers, who are accustomed to state-of-the-art forensic procedures.

Finish your essay in style

You could say:

> In the extract, Holmes is shown to be a logical character through his approach to the investigation, the way that he is described and his language. This impression is reinforced by the way that he is contrasted with other characters in the rest of the novel.

1) This conclusion is okay, but it doesn't go into much detail about <u>how</u> Holmes is presented as logical.

2) So to make it really <u>impressive</u> you could say something like...

> Holmes is presented as a logical character firstly by his rational approach to the mystery, which is demonstrated by his insightful analysis of evidence in the extract and elsewhere in the novel. Holmes's language reinforces this impression: his use of short sentences in the extract illustrates his rapid, reasoned thought processes. However, it is Holmes's contrast with other characters that provides the strongest illustration of his logical character. By encouraging the reader to compare Holmes to characters such as Watson and Jones, Conan Doyle makes Holmes's clear-sightedness and rationality indisputable.

> This shows a reasoned personal opinion about which of Conan Doyle's methods is most effective.

> Make your final sentence really stand out — it's your last opportunity to impress the examiner.

Why do alligators write good essays? Their quotes are so snappy...

It seems like there's a lot to remember on these two pages, but there's not really. To summarise — write a scorching intro and a sizzling conclusion, make a good range of points (one per paragraph) and include plenty of examples. Easy.

Index

The Characters from 'The Sign of the Four'

Phew! You should be an expert on *The Sign of the Four* by now. But if you want a bit of light relief and a quick recap of the novel's plot, sit yourself down and read through *The Sign of the Four — The Cartoon*...

Sherlock Holmes

John Watson

Mary Morstan

Athelney Jones

Thaddeus Sholto

Jonathan Small

Major Sholto

Tonga

Arthur Conan Doyle's 'The Sign of the Four'

ETSF41